T0216361

Implementing SAP S/4HANA

A Framework for Planning and Executing SAP S/4HANA Projects

Sanket Kulkarni

Apress®

Implementing SAP S/4HANA

Sanket Kulkarni
Pune, Maharashtra, India

ISBN-13 (pbk): 978-1-4842-4519-4   ISBN-13 (electronic): 978-1-4842-4520-0
https://doi.org/10.1007/978-1-4842-4520-0

Managing Director, Apress Media LLC: Welmoed Spahr
Acquisitions Editor: Nikhil Karkal
Development Editor: Matthew Moodie
Coordinating Editor: Divya Modi

Cover designed by eStudioCalamar

Cover image designed by Freepik (www.freepik.com)

Distributed to the book trade worldwide by Springer Science+Business Media New York, 233 Spring Street, 6th Floor, New York, NY 10013. Phone 1-800-SPRINGER, fax (201) 348-4505, e-mail orders-ny@springer-sbm.com, or visit www.springeronline.com. Apress Media, LLC is a California LLC and the sole member (owner) is Springer Science + Business Media Finance Inc (SSBM Finance Inc). SSBM Finance Inc is a **Delaware** corporation.

For information on translations, please e-mail rights@apress.com, or visit http://www.apress.com/rights-permissions.

Apress titles may be purchased in bulk for academic, corporate, or promotional use. eBook versions and licenses are also available for most titles. For more information, reference our Print and eBook Bulk Sales web page at http://www.apress.com/bulk-sales.

Any source code or other supplementary material referenced by the author in this book is available to readers on GitHub via the book's product page, located at www.apress.com/978-1-4842-4519-4. For more detailed information, please visit http://www.apress.com/source-code.

Printed on acid-free paper

*To my lovely wife, Archana,
and kids, Rohan and Anika*

Table of Contents

About the Author

Sanket Kulkarni has more than 18 years of experience in implementing SAP solutions worldwide. He has consulted with many customers on complex SAP transformations involving multiyear rollouts. He has worked across a range of industries including consumer goods, oil and gas, semiconductor, and transportation. Over the last few years, he has been coaching customers on SAP S/4HANA-driven digital transformations.

About the Technical Reviewer

Dinesh Mukundu Mohan is a Solution Architect with more than 20 years of IT work experience including 16 years of hands-on SAP experience implementing finance, controlling, planning, consolidation, budgeting, and forecasting solutions using S/4HANA, SAP BPC Optimized for S/4HANA, BPC 11 and 10.1, BW-BPS & IP, and BW and FICO, he has successfully delivered multiple S/4HANA, BPC, and BW implementations and S/4HANA migrations.

He has experience solutioning and enabling clients with decisions on the right range of applications, including S/4HANA, BW4HANA, BPC 10.1, and BPC 11, along with integration of Fiori and BO reporting tools like Lumira 2.X, Design Studio, Analysis for Office 2.X, and Web. His experience extends to working in multiple regions, including North America, Germany, Dubai, Australia, Mexico, Europe, China, and Thailand.

Acknowledgments

In the small world of SAP consulting, you meet two types of people: rocks or rock stars. You know a rock star when you encounter such a person. The rock star is the one who is passionate about SAP, loves helping customers, and is always learning.

This book would not have been possible without the rock stars who shaped my worldview and ignited my passion for SAP throughout my consulting journey. Thank you to Rajesh Ray, Sangeeth Parvatham, Katja Keller, Steffen Bruckner, John Walsh, Christine Kakoti, and Eishvinder Ratra, to name a few.

As they say, it often takes a village to produce a book. Writing is just one portion of it. Thank you to the Apress team (Divya, Nikhil, and Matthew) for professionally handling the rest and making this book happen.

Introduction

SAP released SAP S/4HANA amid much fanfare in February 2015. It demonstrated the promise of the new in-memory computing database HANA, a sleek user interface (UI), Fiori apps, and enhanced functionality. Since then, SAP has improved the S/4HANA suite of products with best practices, industry templates, more than 7,000 Fiori apps, Embedded Analytics, and close integration with Leonardo.

As compared to the SAP ECC system, S/4HANA is a much more advanced enterprise application, well suited for intelligent enterprises. With its leading-edge tool set, possibilities with S/4HANA are limitless. Traditional SAP enterprise resource planning (ERP) systems often excelled at being systems of record. S/4HANA aspires to be a system of intelligence.

What does it mean for organizations embarking on the journey of S/4HANA? How can they plan their journey and not be derailed by the full range of information and choice available?

The days of superspecialization in the SAP space are slowly ending. If you are implementing S/4HANA, you should not only know about the business process, but also the SAP user experience, technical architecture, and cloud offerings, as well as analytics.

So, why did I write this book? Well, the key for successful S/4HANA implementation is developing an all-around view of the components and assess their impact up front. Most of the books or blogs on S/4HANA provide step-by-step information on a very niche topic, leaving you to figure out the big picture yourself. The purpose of this book is to develop the big picture the right way. It is to help you establish a well-rounded understanding of S/4HANA implementation and its associated components. You can always reach out the blogs and SAP help sites for further details.

Who Should Read This Book?

If you are considering SAP S/4HANA, either you are already an SAP customer or planning to be one. As such, I assume that you are familiar with SAP, although you need not be familiar with SAP S/4HANA.

If you are a vital stakeholder or executive who is considering implementing SAP S/4HANA, you will find this book useful, as S/4HANA is going to be the future of SAP as well as your business. This book is the first step in your S/4HANA journey.

How Is This Book Organized?

We begin with the introduction of SAP S/4HANA and discuss the value it brings to the table. We then outline fundamental implementation approaches such as Greenfield and Brownfield at the end of Chapter 1.

The S/4HANA journey starts with an assessment of existing capability vs. the functionality offered by S/4HANA. Chapter 2 discusses various types of assessments done during the planning phases. We then move toward a discussion of the functional aspects of S/4HANA and tools offered by SAP including simplification lists and best practices in Chapter 3.

Once customizations are shortlisted as part of the functional assessment, development is done either through custom code remediations or new SAP objects and apps. We discuss S/4HANA development standards and remediation aspects in Chapter 4.

Data conversion plays a significant role regardless of your implementation approach, whether Greenfield or Brownfield. SAP also offers tools for S/4HANA migration in the case of Brownfield implementations. We discuss data conversion strategy, including extract, transform, and load aspects, in Chapter 5.

Testing is an integral part of every project phase in S/4HANA, beginning in the planning phase. Overall, S/4HANA implementation is testing intensive, with various cycles being run in parallel—regression, performance, integration testing, and so on. Chapter 6 discusses a variety of test cycles and dependencies among them.

Migration to a cloud infrastructure is often combined with S/4HANA implementation. Various technical architecture aspects such as sizing, datacenter management, S/4HANA migration, and security are discussed in Chapter 7.

S/4HANA changes organizations in many ways. Organization change management (OCM) is often sidelined as organizations struggle with low rates of user adoption and subsequent delays in deployment. Chapter 8 presents you with various approaches to improve user adoption and change management.

SAP Fiori is one of the key value propositions of S/4HANA. Chapter 9 discusses the Fiori architecture, ways to implement Fiori apps, and methods for customizing it.

Embedded Analytics offers real-time reporting via analytical apps. Views developed using Embedded Analytics can also be accessed by other reporting applications. Chapter 10 touches on an SAP analytics strategy and how Embedded Analytics can help.

S/4HANA implementation is one of the most important IT projects you will ever run. It requires proper considerations of program governance and deployment strategy. We discuss many options for deployment and program governance in Chapter 11.

All of this information culminates in the business case for S/4HANA. It is an objective assessment of the effort it takes to implement vis-à-vis the benefits it brings. Chapter 12 offers you guidelines to develop and manage a business case for S/4HANA implementation.

Finally, Chapter 13 discusses some unique aspects of S/4HANA implementation if you are going for a central finance implementation or S/4HANA on the cloud.

All of the topics covered deserve a separate book by themselves if explored in detail. As stated earlier, the purpose of this book is to help you develop a navigational map for S/4HANA implementation, rather than spoon-feed you every step.

From Here

In the third century BC, Greek writer Plutarch put it best when he wrote, "Mind is not a vessel to be filled, rather a spark to be lighted." I hope that as a reader of this book, you embark on the S/4HANA journey with a quiet confidence that comes only from your knowledge. I hope you enjoy the book.

CHAPTER 1

SAP S/4HANA Overview

How would you like to trade your old enterprise resource planning (ERP) system—SAP or non-SAP—for a sleek new SAP S/4HANA implementation? It is not a yes-or-no question anymore. The question is not "why," but instead it is about "how." That does not mean that you should forget why altogether. Rather, it is important to consider the why of SAP S/4HANA before the hows. The purpose of this book is to circumvent all the marketing behind SAP S/4HANA; you probably have had enough of it over the last few years. The purpose is to help you with insightful action, making an educated decision and executing your SAP S/4HANA business case seamlessly. The purpose is to get the big picture on SAP S/4HANA right and leave the details to the experts and subject matter experts (SMEs) who specialize in particular scope areas. It should help you build a strong SAP S/4HANA implementation framework (or tool set) supported by a strong business case. If you eventually get excited about the new era with SAP S/4HANA while being reasonably confident in your ability to execute, then I would say that the book has served its purpose.

The first question is why someone would want to move to SAP S/4HANA. As you survey your existing ERP landscape, you see a highly customized system well-tuned to your way of conducting business. It is like a made-for-each-other system, working just for you. Reasons to migrate can be distilled down to two broad-based drivers. To be clear, it is not only

© Sanket Kulkarni 2019
S. Kulkarni, *Implementing SAP S/4HANA*, https://doi.org/10.1007/978-1-4842-4520-0_1

about the innovations or sleek UI or faster reporting that comes along with SAP S/4HANA. It is rather about your way of doing business and how it will be changed by technology and business forces in the future.

As you would agree, the last ten years have been somewhat pathbreaking for the technology industry. Cloud computing came into the mainstream as early as 2006. That was followed by mobile computing, then big data analytics, as computing power became cheap and on demand. On the enterprise systems side, the proliferation of cloud services and better tools for rapid prototyping has reduced the time between idea and execution. Software-as-a-Service (SaaS) offerings were built specifically into these developments, so it is now possible to get best-in-class enterprise tools in seconds. The ubiquity of cloud vendors means that your infrastructure can be hosted anywhere and be scaled in a matter of days.

On the IT project execution side, the waterfall was the norm by which ERP projects were delivered. It took a long time before even end users could see the final product. Collaborative philosophies like Agile and DevOps have now become the norm. These enabled faster, user-centric developments across the enterprise space.

By far the most important factor is that technology has become ubiquitous. With the power of mobile handsets, customers quickly moved to mobile-centric applications to buy, compare, and rate. End customers and users expect a rich technology experience anytime, anywhere. The way they interact with your organization has completely changed. The ways you buy, sell, and stock goods have changed due to these technology drivers.

If your customers have moved ahead of the technology curve, would your existing ERP remain behind? If the pace of the technology changes continues, then you will need a new-age ERP system that is easy to scale, cloud-native, and more user-centric than ever. That's where SAP S/4HANA fits in. Even if you forget marketing rhetoric for a bit, there is a bit of truth in saying that so far, your ERP system has been acting as a system-of-record. With SAP S/4HANA, you can make it a system-of-innovation. With a faster computing HANA database that can be hosted on the cloud, improved user experience via role-based, responsive Fiori apps, and real-time reporting, it is now much easier to generate operational insights on the go.

SAP, as the leading ERP vendor, has been observing technology trends from the front lines. Since the days of the mainframe-centric SAP R1 in 1972, SAP has always been interested in finding faster, more efficient ways for the ERP application layer to communicate with the ERP database layer. This led to multiple models such as client/server architecture with SAP R/3, service-oriented architecture, and then early experiments with HANA, in-memory computing with Business Suite on HANA (SOH) in 2013. SAP Simple Finance followed in 2014 and then the full ERP suite of products evolved, what we call SAP S/4HANA henceforth.

New in SAP S/4HANA

So, what has changed with SAP S/4HANA? The next sections cover the new features.

New Architecture

SAP S/4HANA operates on top of HANA using the new concept of in-memory tables, with simplified data models and embedded analytics. Time-consuming processes, such as period-end closing, can now be done on the fly. It eliminates reconciliation efforts between functional areas such as Finance, Procurement, Production and Sales. It gives you real-time analytical reporting based on Embedded Analytics.

Process Simplification

Although most of the product functionality in has been retained, there is new way to look at the processes with the redesign of tables along with available best practices. For example, Universal Journal in the SAP finance area has led to much better reporting and much needed simplification.

New User Experience

This is supplied via SAP Fiori or self-service tools like Lumira. SAP S/4HANA has introduced role-based apps accessible via smartphones, tablets, and desktops.

Deployment Choice

SAP S/4HANA comes with On-Premise and Cloud editions. You can have the On-Premise edition hosted on cloud, thus reaping the benefits of your existing cloud vendor relationships. Cloud-native ERP such SAP S/4HANA will mean that its scalable, application programming interface (API)-driven by design.

Summary of Changes

Please note that I refer the On-Premise Edition of SAP S/4HANA for all discussion purposes, but the majority of this information would also apply to SAP S/4HANA Cloud Edition as well. There are two separate product development tracks managed by SAP:

- 1809 is the latest On-Premise Edition.

- 1902 is the latest Cloud Edition.

Quarterly upgrades are the norm in the Cloud Edition, whereas yearly upgrades (optional) are a norm for the On-Premise Edition. Three successive

Feature Pack Stacks (FPSs) are released on a quarterly basis for the On-Premise Edition, which typically include nondisruptive or mandatory features.

Table 1-1 provides a quick summary of the changes implemented in SAP S/4HANA as compared to your existing SAP ERP instance.

Table 1-1. *Changes in SAP S/4HANA*

	SAP S/4HANA	**SAP Business Suite**
Data model	Simplified – ¾ objects reduced	Traditional
Database	HANA DB	Any DB
Fiori apps	7,000+ as of date	50 (if DB is HANA)
Non-SAP ERP components (EWM, TM, APO)	Merged in S/4HANA core functionality	Separate systems
Programming language	ABAP	ABAP
Embedded Analytics	CDS (Core Data Services) Views	HANA Live

What Is in IT for Me?

That is always a valid question. SAP S/4HANA is often the biggest endeavor in an IT organization given the scale, impact on business, and complexity of it. How can you be confident that you have the skill sets as well as an appetite to execute such a program? It all starts with defining the business case of SAP S/4HANA.

The benefits of implementing SAP S/4HANA are obvious:

- Reduction in customizations as it encourages a fit-to-standard approach, thus reducing the burden on the organization to maintain and enhance it further.

- Better operational insights via Embedded Analytics.

- Faster business adoption with the rich UI via Fiori apps.

- Faster period-end closing due to better financial and management reporting via functionalities like Universal Journal.

- Better supply chain functionalities with embedded Transportation Management (TM) and Enterprise Warehouse Management (EWM).

When you build a business case, these benefits have to be factored into the numbers. These numbers will eventually justify the investment you will make to implement SAP S/4HANA; this takes up the "how" question.

If you have carefully read through the discussion of technology trends in the last few pages, it might have already dawned on you that the way you will implement SAP S/4HANA will be far different than the last time you implemented your ERP systems. The method you will use to conduct the blueprinting exercise, build and test the system, and deploy it to the cloud is an all-new way of working for your organization, and so it needs to be clearly understood. Once you have a clear understanding of all the scope areas, you will eventually do a bottom-up cost analysis. It will then be fed into the SAP S/4HANA business.

So, you get your costs on the right and benefits on the left. That has what we have been talking about the business case so far.

Now you would ask how does it help me in execution? Well, a clear understanding of what it entails to implement SAP S/4HANA should give you better handle in planning and managing the implementation project, thus better chance of meeting the business case.

How Should I Go About It?

You can approach the SAP S/4HANA journey in multiple ways. Factors driving the decision are as follows.

- What is your starting point? Do you have an existing SAP ERP system or non-SAP ERP system? It is rather straightforward. If you are starting from the SAP base, you can migrate from old the SAP ERP to a new SAP S/4HANA implementation. For non-SAP, it is always a brand new SAP S/4HANA implementation.

- How customized is your ERP system? It is often a good indicator of complexity inherent in your business processes. Sometimes this is determined just by the nature of the industry you are in; for example, validation requirements in the pharmaceutical industry or complex available-to-promise (ATP) scenarios in the aftermarket industry. Sometimes it's just the factor of continuing the same-old system, thus an opportunity to go back to standard instead.

- Do you have a single instance of SAP ERP across the organization or multiple instances, thus making the case for instance consolidation?

- How much of your data—master and transaction included—would you like to carry over to SAP S/4HANA? As part of the clean-up act, you might want to consider organizational elements you no longer use; for example, if you have closed a sales office in the country and do not need to have one, perhaps that data could be cleaned up.

SAP S/4HANA Implementation

There are essentially two broad-based approaches for your SAP S/4HANA journey.

- Greenfield.

- Brownfield.

Greenfield Implementation

Greenfield implementation is about starting from scratch, on a blank slate. This gives your organization the opportunity to reengineer, going back to standard. You use best practices to a great extent, do away with old antiquated practices, and boldly step into new ways of working. That does not mean that you do not have to perform data conversion, but you do it based on intelligent selection. Only relevant data gets converted to the SAP S/4HANA data model either manually or programmatically. The rest of the data is either archived or deleted.

Depending on the SAP S/4HANA version you opt for, your modus operandi for implementation will change. Although SAP S/4HANA On-Premise or Cloud Edition (single tenant) enable customizations an extent, Cloud Edition (multitenant) enforces best practices and strict data formatting guidelines.

You would opt for the Greenfield option in the following cases:

- Your current business processes are suboptimal and the data design is outdated.

- You have many instances of ERPs that you want to consolidate in a single instance.

- There is a low tolerance for customizations and higher inclination for leveraging standard SAP processes and best practices (without customization).

- Your organization is willing to invest significant effort into reengineering and optimizing all business processes and change management that follows.

Brownfield Implementation

Brownfield implementation is all about converting your existing SAP ERP system to SAP S/4HANA. There is obviously less process remapping effort, but a lot of effort goes into data mapping and conversion and the associated testing. SAP provides tools for data conversion that expedite this process to a certain extent. Depending on the degree of customization and volume of data, the Brownfield mplementation project can take a long time to realize.

Such a project involves detailed fit-gap analysis in functional, technical, and architectural areas. It leads to a specific migration or conversion path to SAP S/4HANA. There are some variants to the Brownfield approach apart from wholesale Brownfield conversion.

- Implementation of Central Finance to integrate with existing SAP ERP first, then implementation of the rest of the SAP S/4HANA functionalities.

- Implementation of S/4HANA Finance (finance functionalities only) while existing ERPs continue to support nonfinance functionalities as they are slowly moved to SAP S/4HANA.

- Migration of the existing SAP ERP system to Business Suite on HANA, then to SAP S/4HANA. This approach is only considered when you have an old version of the SAP ECC system and would like to have the innovation brought by HANA Database, to begin with.

You would opt for Brownfield in the following cases.

- Current business processes are up to date, optimized, and meet the needs of the business.

- Architecture is fully optimized (e.g., a single instance of SAP globally).

- You can manage risks associated with data conversion effectively either by working with SAP or in-house skills.

- You are not interested in investing significant effort in reengineering and optimizing all business processes. This leads to less effort in change management but more effort in redesigning your existing customizations into the new data model, data conversion, and associated testing.

Typically, you will start with an SAP S/4HANA assessment, taking stock of the existing ERP landscape in terms of existing customizations and potential gaps in functionalities as well as architecture. You will also look at cloud strategy, and whether you have existing relationships with cloud vendors or they need to be developed. The SAP S/4HANA implementation approach often ties into your infrastructure and cloud strategy, so it is important to align them to begin with. Depending on your inclination to invest hard work in business transformation or data conversion and migration, you can choose your migration path to SAP S/4HANA in terms of Greenfield or Brownfield.

The next task at hand is to gather all the inputs for building the business case. It is also called solutioning, the process of estimating and monitoring your ERP project. It is a way of reasonably arriving at estimates and converting those estimates into the staffing plan. This is the process we use to build estimates and arrive at the baseline staffing plan to establish a budget for the project. It is based on certain assumptions and gives key performance indicators against which you should measure the success of the project.

In traditional custom software development projects, organizations use something called function-point analysis or a lines-of-code-based estimation process that not only drives development, but also testing effort. In the world of packaged software like SAP S/4HANA, such a concept is not useful. In that case, how do you reliably estimate and build a business case? As expected, there are a variety of scope areas involved in the SAP S/4HANA project, such as functional, development, and testing to name a few. It is important to get a clear understanding of what each area entails as far SAP S/4HANA implementation is concerned and then find a way to estimate the same. Some organizations go with a full-time equivalent (FTE) model where they think about the resources needed to get the work done. Some develop sophisticated estimating guidelines to measure development or testing effort. How good your estimation models are might depend on the maturity of your IT organization. Because SAP S/4HANA will be a one-of-a-kind project for your organization, the learning curve is expected to be steep for both IT as well as business, so any estimation model you choose should have adequate contingency built in. Such models should be flexible to adjust to new sets of information you encounter during the project and still have broad-based rules to abide by.

In upcoming chapters, you will see wide-ranging discussion on each of these scope areas in terms of how SAP S/4HANA projects are executed and measured. As you get through each of these chapters, an estimation framework should emerge starting with scope assumptions for each scope area, key data points driving the effort, like number of reports, interfaces, conversions, enhancements, forms, and workflows (RICEFWs), number of mock conversions, and so on. These factors should drive your estimation models and help with developing a business case in terms of timeline, migration approach and, cost–benefit analysis.

Any organization embarking on an SAP S/4HANA journey should have an eye toward the future. Organizations are looking for automation, artificial intelligence, machine learning, or even blockchain to make better and insightful decisions, to understand and serve customers better, and to gain a competitive advantage. With SAP Leonardo working with SAP S/4HANA and associated intelligent enterprise themes, the future sure looks exciting. It is time not to be afraid, but to be excited.

Additional References

- https://open.sap.com/
- http://discover.sap.com/S4HANA
- https://help.sap.com/s4hana
- https://scn.sap.com/docs/DOC-64980

CHAPTER 2

Scope Areas of SAP S/4HANA

So you want to embark on SAP S/4HANA journey, and of course you intend to make it a success. Obviously, it will be one of the largest IT transformations in your organization. You might ve overwhelmed by the enormity of the task at hand. You feel like implementing ERP all over again, with the same concerns around managing multiyear rollouts across different geographies or interfacing with your business partners.

The value proposition of SAP S/4HANA from the business perspective is very attractive in terms of intelligent enterprise, the sleek Fiori UI, Embedded Analytics, and potential Leonardo capabilities for machine learning or artificial intelligence. It is a big change in the way you do business, in terms of how you procure, manufacture, and even sell to customers. Such a digital transformation can be overwhelming, no matter how much experience you already have.

The big question is this: How does one plan for a successful SAP S/4HANA implementation project? Treating it like a business transformation instead of just another ERP project can be a good starting point. It also means that set precedents or experience (you might call it a gut feeling) are not going to help much.

What you are looking for is some sort of framework covering all the areas involved in SAP S/4HANA implementation. For each of these areas, you should be aware of the implementation approach along with key input

© Sanket Kulkarni 2019
S. Kulkarni, *Implementing SAP S/4HANA*, https://doi.org/10.1007/978-1-4842-4520-0_2

and output data points driving such considerations. The advantage of such a data-driven approach is delivery certainty and much better control over the outcome. At the same time, such a framework does offer you ways to customize per your unique requirements in each of the scope areas. Over the next chapters, we will go through each of these scope areas in detail, making sure that you get the big picture right while enabling you to work on the nitty-gritty as you like. Let us dive into it, beginning with a listing of various scope areas associated with SAP S/4HANA implementation.

Creating the Implementation Framework

Any ERP implementation framework involves three simple steps.

1. Identify scope areas (e.g., development).

2. Identify drivers for estimating the effort. For example, you already know that drivers of any SAP development effort are a number of RICEFWs. If you know the unit effort to develop and test each one of them, you will get a good handle on the projected effort.

3. Monitor the scope area during project execution. Monitoring involves the "real" number of RICEFWs encountered during the project. If you are close to the number initially estimated, there is a high probability that development will be proceed as per the plan.

Although it might sound simple in principle, thus far there is no readily available framework on the market. You can build one by yourself, though, using the principles from this book. The first step in that direction is SAP S/4HANA assessment.

The objective for the SAP S/4HANA assessment exercise is to calibrate how well you know your business (and associated ERP aspects) in terms of important customizations and how they will transform as you switch to SAP S/4HANA. There are also additional considerations regarding scalability, often tied to upcoming mergers and acquisitions or agility and managing multiple cloud partner relationships and their impact on your ERP infrastructure.

SAP S/4HANA assessment is an opportunity for you to assess the following:

- As-is scenario: This details how do you do business, manage infrastructure, or develop extensions.

- To-be scenario: In this scenario, you visualize how things will change as you move to SAP S/4HANA. Your SAP UI might change to SAP Fiori, reporting might change to Embedded Analytics, or the development process might be simplified.

- What it takes: This involves planning the transition, developing estimation models up front, and monitoring progress closely.

In summary, SAP S/4HANA assessment is the process of laying out the roadmap for your SAP S/4HANA journey.

Your starting point is to gather as much information as you can about the existing ERP system in terms of current processes—active, obsolete, or soon-to-be obsolete ones—customizations, development standards, infrastructure considerations, technical architecture landscape, and so on. The objective is to cover all scope areas, whether they are affected or not, as part of the scope assessment.

Functional Impact Assessment

A leading concern for organizations embarking on this journey is the impact on the business. Will it change the way you do business? How will it affect your partners, customers and vendors alike? To what extent can you adopt SAP best practices without sacrificing unique aspects of the business? Several questions arise up front as you look at SAP S/4HANA. Such concerns can be addressed by conducting what I call business process assessment. Regardless of the specific implementation approach you choose, Greenfield or Brownfield, business process assessment is an absolute must.

In this activity, you start by looking at your existing business processes and how they are currently modeled in the ERP system. If you have business process maps, they will come in handy, too. Next, start shortlisting critical business processes in each of the functional areas and dive deep in terms of listing out legal, regulatory, and strategic considerations. Most likely, such considerations have already driven customization in your current ERP landscape, and such customizations also need to be carried out in the SAP S/4HANA implementation as well.

Armed with this information, you can start doing workshops for each functional area and conducting a high-level impact analysis. Functional impact analysis is the process of mapping your functional processes (mainly critical ones) against the SAP S/4HANA simplification list. SAP lists all S/4HANA-related changes there and often advises all client to look through the simplification list, to assess process-level fit for their business. For noncritical processes, you can look to adopt SAP best practices with minimal customization. It is an opportunity to further simplify your business processes, eliminating of antiquated ones, adopting best practices, and allowing customizations for only critical ones. We discuss various aspects of functional impact assessment in Chapter 3.

Technical Impact Assessment

Once you have an idea about the degree of customizations needed, you can conduct a technical impact assessment. Your implementation approach will drive most of the considerations in the technical area. Particularly if you are leaning toward Brownfield conversion, you will be interested to carry your existing customizations into the SAP S/4HANA system. This is done via a process called custom code remediation, by which your existing custom code is made to work in the new S/4HANA-based environment.

SAP can run a readiness check for you through which you can understand the impact to your custom code. You would start with determining how much customization you have in your current system, listing custom objects in your namespace. Then, you can use the SAP readiness check tools to see whether this code needs to be changed in the SAP S/4HANA version. Generally, there are two levels of changes needed in your custom programs.

- Changes needed to database queries because SAP S/4HANA runs on the HANA database with a simplified table structure.

- Changes needed as per new functionalities.

For Greenfield implementations, technical considerations are driven by the degree of customization needed, often identified by a number of RICEFWs. We discuss technical impact assessment in greater detail in Chapter 4.

Data Impact Assessment

Data is the most critical aspect of your SAP S/4HANA project. You need a deliberate data conversion strategy depending on the implementation approach you choose. Brownfield conversions often involve transferring data from your old SAP ERP system to SAP S/4HANA. As table structures are different than the current SAP ERP system, data needs to be transformed and loaded to SAP S/4HANA. For Brownfield conversions, SAP provides tools to transform and load the data. For Greenfield implementations, considerations are the same as for any ERP project in terms of extraction from a legacy system, transforming the data, and loading it.

As part of the data impact assessment, you need to first understand the state of your data. As is the case for any ERP system that has been live for so long, there is a lot of data that can be archived or is not at all needed for the conversion. You can identify data objects for conversion and the associated volume of data. You might even consider data harmonization if you are bringing data into SAP S/4HANA from multiple legacy systems, as is often the case with SAP consolidation or SAP S/4HANA central finance projects. You should also discuss a number of mock conversions and their impact on other project phases such as testing, cutover, and so on. As part of data impact assessment, you are looking to simplify your data landscape as you move to SAP S/4HANA. We discuss this further in Chapter 5.

Test Assessment

Testing is often most the underrated but most important area of your SAP S/4HANA project. Although there will be a tendency to embed it into the respective process or development teams, you should focus on test planning up front. The primary objective of testing should be ensuring that things work in the same fashion as they did in your legacy ERP system. Whether you are opting for a Greenfield or Brownfield implementation approach, the testing approach remains the same. You should be testing the entire functionality end-to-end, including interfaces. Performance benchmarks in your legacy ERP system should also be retained as you move to the new SAP S/4HANA system. As part of test assessment, you plan various test cycles at the start: system integration testing, performance testing, user acceptance testing, and so on. Based on the functional and technical assessments, you will already have a handle on customizations carried forward to the SAP S/4HANA instance. It also drives the overall test scope. With Fiori being the key UI component, test planning also covers necessary testing (both functionality in Fiori Apps and performance across devices). We discuss various aspects of testing for your SAP S/4HANA project in Chapter 6.

Technical Architecture Assessment

Often confused with infrastructure and cloud migrations, technical architecture in SAP S/4HANA is all about having the optimal technical landscape. It includes conversations around sizing, datacenter policies, and high availability/disaster recovery (HA/DR) considerations. For Brownfield implementations, you should also discuss a dual landscape, having production still on the old SAP ERP and the project landscape on SAP S/4HANA during the project life cycle. As part of the technical architecture assessment, respective retrofit strategies also need to be outlined because changes in the production landscape should be retrofitted in the SAP S/4HANA project landscape eventually. There is also a specific technical migration path to be discussed from the start as you move from SAP ERP to the SAP S/4HANA instance. Your technical architecture assessment starts with understanding your current SAP landscape along with existing infrastructure and technical architecture requirements. Such requirements also include setting up Fiori servers. Your existing relationships with cloud vendors will also have a bearing on the architecture. As part of the assessment, internal security team requirements are also mentioned in detail. Policies, certificates, and IT authorization strategy should be aligned.

The technical architecture assessment leads to the generation of the bill of materials (BOM), a laundry list of every SAP system in your landscape with a view toward potential SAP S/4HANA migration. We discuss more about this in Chapter 7.

Organizational Change Management Assessment

Often ignored, organizational change management (OCM) is the most important area in your SAP S/4HANA implementation. With simplification driving the implementation agenda, business and user buy-ins are required throughout the project whether you want to adopt best practices or discuss Fiori UI strategy. OCM assessment involves detailing various aspects of communications and stakeholder management. If there are any job role changes involved, OCM also focuses on reskilling or job design aspects. Training is often included as part of this assessment. It involves detailing user training strategy in terms of train-the-trainer sessions, development of training materials, user instructions, or standard operating procedures. Training delivery in terms of locations, method (classroom, interactive, or web-based) is also discussed up front. We discuss OCM and training aspects in more detail in Chapter 8.

SAP UX (Fiori) Assessment

Fiori UI is the unique aspect of your SAP S/4HANA implementation. Designing and enabling the SAP UI (either via Fiori or any other SAP UX technologies) require upfront planning and assessment. The process requires deliberate consideration to assess your SAP UI requirements and conduct analysis of available FIORI apps. Fiori apps come in different variants: transactional, analytical, or fact-sheets. It therefore becomes important to understand UI design aspects as part of the Fiori assessment. Customization requirements for the SAP UI need to be thought through, as Fiori might not be the right answer for your every UI requirement. We discuss this topic further in Chapter 9.

SAP Analytics Assessment

SAP S/4HANA comes with a set of prepackaged analytics in terms of Embedded Analytics or analytical Fiori apps. Although most of your operational reporting requirements are covered by it, the SAP analytics assessment focuses on a broader analytics strategy, in terms of operational, tactical, and strategic reporting. Embedded Analytics might be the right answer for deriving actionable insights from real-time operational reporting, but tactical and strategic reporting can still reside in your enterprise data warehouse (EDW). The SAP analytics assessment takes a holistic view of your reporting requirements and conducts an analysis on available SAP S/4HANA reporting functionalities offered by Embedded Analytics. Customizations can be outlined at the start to meet specific reporting requirements by evaluating technologies on offer—SAP Fiori analytical apps, Embedded Analytics, and so on. We talk more about SAP analytics assessment in Chapter 10.

Contrary to traditional SAP ERP implementations, SAP S/4HANA implementations need an all-encompassing view on each of the scope areas listed here. As you might have noticed already, as part of these assessments, your objective should be to get the big picture right before you embark on your SAP S/4HANA journey.

CHAPTER 3

Process Effort in S/4HANA

The primary objective of the process teams is to develop and execute a business case for SAP S/4HANA. They are continually engaged throughout the S/4HANA implementation, acting as a bridge between business stakeholders and project teams.

During the planning and assessment phase, process effort is focussed on conducting workshops with business stakeholders, developing a business case. Based on the fit-gap analysis, a list of customizations is identified. Then, a detailed functional design helps in the preparation of functional and configuration specifications.

Customizations are built along with the development teams during the build phase. Process teams then execute various cycles of testing, starting with unit testing, then system integration testing, regression testing, and so on.

After successful execution of the test phase, process teams work with business stakeholders during the final cutover. Cutover activities include the transfer of configuration, customizations to the production system, and migration of master and transaction data. Process teams also participate in data validation and production simulation cycles during cutover. Process effort is spent throughout the project and is crucial for the success of the overall program.

© Sanket Kulkarni 2019
S. Kulkarni, *Implementing SAP S/4HANA*, https://doi.org/10.1007/978-1-4842-4520-0_3

Process Assessment

Being an enterprise application, SAP S/4HANA is expected to deliver real business benefits. Business benefits are often tied to the process improvements brought together by specific SAP S/4HANA capabilities. The objective of the process assessment is to identify critical SAP S/4HANA capabilities that have the potential to deliver specific business benefits. This exercise is often twofold:

- Work with business to understand pain points and improvement areas.

- Understand SAP S/4HANA capabilities that either reduce the pain or improve business operations substantially, thus delivering benefits.

Process assessment begins with the process visioning exercise. Such an exercise helps you outline critical challenges in a process area along with SAP S/4HANA capabilities. Once capabilities are shortlisted based on the value they bring to the table, deep-dive workshops are held. Each capability is then split further into subtopics, which are then compared against a simplification items list as well as SAP best practices. Process fit-gaps are later identified and converted into the list of customizations to be developed. Such customizations are further categorized into RICEFWs and fed into the development area.

We next explain various activities involved in the process assessment by taking an example of finance, the most common process area across organizations.

Identify Core Processes and Architecture

In this section, you identify critical business processes and define the as-is and to-be process architectures for each process area.

- Identify core processes

  - Core business processes for each area are identified up front. For example, you start by identifying core finance processes:

    - Finance master data

    - Business planning and consolidation

    - Financial accounting: Accounts payable, receivable

    - Intercompany accounting

    - Taxation

    - Treasury

    - Compliance

    - Reporting and analytics

  - There are also touchpoints with other process areas. Process ownership for each touchpoint has to be identified up front. For example, finance is integrated with the supply chain function for sales and operations planning. Ownership is with the supply chain function, though.

- Define as-is and to-be architecture

  - As-is architecture involves defining a system landscape covering core business process areas. To-be architecture describes a system landscape once SAP S/4HANA is implemented.

25

- Your architecture might involve separate systems for consolidation, taxation, and treasury, as well as reporting. You might also have an outsourced payroll function that needs to be integrated.

- The to-be architecture can include moving these functions—Consolidation, Taxation, Treasury, and Reporting—to SAP S/4HANA while retaining an outsourced payroll function.

Understanding Process Vision

A process visioning exercise helps you identify various process improvement opportunities that can be enabled by moving to SAP S/4HANA.

- You begin a visioning workshop for each process by gathering data on the following:

    - Existing organizational structure and entities

    - Current issues and pain points

    - Current improvement programs and initiatives

    - Business wish list or vision that gets translated into opportunities

    - Key performance indicators (KPIs) and business metrics

- For example, you might aspire to move finance operations from just bookkeeping and statutory reporting to analytics-driven value-added activities.

- You are looking to reduce the cost of finance operations by enabling SAP S/4HANA capabilities such as Universal Journal, Embedded Analytics, and Embedded Master Data Governance.

- The business metric to be tracked is cost of finance as percentage of sales. You measure it as 2% of sales.

- Current pain points are antiquated ERP, significant manual effort, and large volume of transactions.

- With SAP S/4HANA, manual effort in day-to-day transactions such as data entry and reconciliation is reduced. Month-end closing happens much faster due to real-time accounting and automated processes.

- You look for industry benchmarks such as APQC/SAP Value Manager and figure that in your industry, cost of finance as percentage of sales is 1% of sales. With SAP S/4HANA, you can thus reduce finance operations costs in line with benchmarks and derive business benefits. Such information is fed into the business case evaluation exercise.

- Once all the opportunities in the process areas are identified, prioritization is done by doing a cost–benefit analysis. Opportunities on the top of the list are the ones offering better return on investment (ROI): higher business benefits vs. lower costs of implementation.

- Some opportunities can also be cross-functional, such as merger and acquisitions integration or analytics.

- For example, SAP S/4HANA capabilities such as Embedded Analytics dashboards are useful for analytics functions used in the finance area. An analytics initiative, however, could be driven separately at the program level.

- Some areas like merger and acquisitions integrations can be addressed by creating an integration playbook for legal and tax entity setup, rather than any specific SAP S/4HANA capability.

Understanding SAP S/4HANA Capabilities

Once various improvement opportunities are identified, they are mapped to multiple SAP S/4HANA capabilities. As part of this exercise, you also define the target business process model and associated SAP S/4HANA components. A sample representation for the finance process area is shown in Table 3-1.

Table 3-1. *Target Business Process Model*

Process Area	Finance Master Data	Business Planning	Reporting & Analytics
S/4HANA Component	S/4HANA	SAP BPC	S/4HANA, SAP BPC
Process capabilities	Legal entity structure	Strategic planning	Management allocations
	Universal Journal	Planning & budgeting	Cost accounting
	Chart of accounts	Forecasting	Management reporting
	Additional accounting dimensions		Fiori and Embedded Analytics

Each of these process capabilities is better understood by tools such as the simplification list or SAP best practices.

Simplification List

The simplification list is the starting point to understanding various solution capabilities in SAP S/4HANA on a process level. It is especially important when you plan to pursue a Brownfield SAP S/4HANA migration from an existing SAP ERP system.

The simplification list is a collection of individual simplification items. Each simplification item contains the following information.

- Description.

- Business impact.

- Recommendations.

- SAP notes (for related prechecks or custom code checks).

The simplification list might look long because it covers the entire set of capabilities of SAP S/4HANA, including industry solutions. Based on those capabilities, you can focus on simplification items.

It is a handy document because it covers all of the process-level changes introduced by SAP as part of the SAP S/4HANA suite.

- For example, you might find more details about the Finance Data Model changes under the Universal Journal section.

- From multiple financial tables with redundant data, SAP has moved to a single table ACDOCA with more than 350 columns in SAP S/4HANA. The purpose is to create a single source of truth by having a separate line item table with full details for all applications, enabling instant insight and extensibility. Among the benefits of such an approach are, data is stored only once. Thus, no reconciliation is needed by design. It also makes multidimensional reporting possible without replicating data to the Enterprise Data Warehouse (EDW).

Best Practices

SAP best practices are predefined business processes modeled for SAP S/4HANA. Each SAP best practice contains the following information:

- Predefined processes.

- Test scripts.

- Process flows.

- Configuration guides.

Based on the SAP S/4HANA edition, On-Premise or Cloud or Industry solutions, you can filter best practices. SAP best practices are useful when you have highly customized business processes and want to move toward standardization.

For example, the financial operations process has an SAP best practice, Accounts Payable (J60), for managing open invoices created from purchasing processes. It covers the process flow as follows.

- Manage and complete supplier master data.

- Create an invoice from logistics.

- Analyze outstanding payables.

- Pay invoice.

- Approve payments (optional).

- Forward payments to banks via SAP Financial Services Network (FSN) or download payment file.

- Analyze the efficiency of payment processing.

Mapping S/4HANA Capabilities

Going through the simplification list and best practices gives you an idea about the extent of SAP S/4HANA capabilities. There are also crucial master data changes affecting process areas as follows:

- The material length has been extended to 40 characters. Although all related SAP development entities (domain, structures, data tables) are adjusted in SAP S/4HANA, the impact on interfaces has to be considered.

- SAP S/4HANA has introduced the concept of a Business Partner Universal account that plays multiple roles within the organization. It means that the separate customer and vendor master are no longer used. This has implications for master data maintenance for certain process areas.

The next step is to map opportunities identified during the process visioning exercise to the SAP S/4HANA capabilities. You might consider multiple options to enable such capability and evaluate the pros and cons of each one of them. Such analysis is then further distilled down into key design decisions, which act as guidelines for all detailed design discussions. Table 3-2 shows you a representation of such an analysis for the finance process area.

Table 3-2. *Opportunity S/4HANA Capability Mapping*

Process	Opportunity	S/4HANA Capability Options	Pros	Cons
Reporting and Analytics	Real-time reporting and predictive analytics	Continue use of external reporting tool	Common view across the organization	Data latency
		Leverage S/4HANA Embedded Analytics	Real-time information	Need to maintain S/4 analytics and external data reporting tool during deployments
Consolidations	Real-time financial consolidations	Continue in the external consolidation tool	No change in the business processes * No user training	Limitation on the business planning options Impact on the interfaces due to change in data models
		Use BPC for consolidation in combination with central finance from non-S/4HANA entities	Real-time information	Implementation and training effort (new application design, interface)

Credit Management	New Credit Management in FSCM	Credit management functionality moved to FSCM module with S/4HANA 1610	Simple data models New credit management functionalities	New configuration and training efforts
Material Ledger	Standard Material Ledger	Use of material ledger with Universal Journal entries	Simple data model and processes Multiple valuation approach and transfer price	Implementation and training effort (new application design, interface)
Business Partner Approach	Adopt a Business Partner approach with customer or vendor integration; also affects sales, procurement	Business partner concept mandatory with S/4HANA	New data models and business processes for accounts payable and accountsreceivable	Implementation and training effort (new application design, interface)

33

The simplification list item and best practices for each capability are identified. Then, each capability is assessed for an impact across the following various areas:

- Process impact.

- Data impact.

- Configuration impact.

- Security impact.

- Integration impact.

- OCM impact.

- Cutover impact.

For example, you are looking at the SAP S/4HANA capability of data model changes in finance area as a simplification item. It is related to the Universal Journal entries, thus removal of compatibility views, total, and index tables. This change affects all financial transactions. Let us assess the impact of this change across the areas given earlier.

- Process impact

    - No impact because this is a purely technical change.

- Data impact

    - Customizing, including open line items, and GL (General Ledger) balances are migrated using standard SAP data tools. Data impact is high due to the volume as well as the number of iterations involved.

- Configuration impact

- No impact because this is a purely technical change.
- Security impact
    - No impact to security roles.
- Integration impact
    - No impact because it is not relevant for integration to non-SAP systems.
- OCM impact
    - Users have to be trained on Universal Journal and related concepts.
- Cutover impact
    - High impact due to high-volume conversion and postcutover validation steps involved.

Based on this analysis, you decide on the list of SAP S/4HANA capabilities to be enabled for each process area along with the customizations needed.

Conclusion

In summary, the process assessment for SAP S/4HANA is performed as shown here.

- You identify core processes for each process area along with the as-is and to-be architectures.
- Then, you conduct the visioning exercise, which considers current pain points and ongoing initiatives. Multiple opportunities are identified for process improvements by leveraging SAP S/4HANA

capabilities. They are then prioritized based on the cost–benefit analysis.

- SAP S/4HANA capabilities are then detailed using available information from the simplification list as well as SAP S/4HANA best practices. They are further mapped to the process improvement opportunities identified earlier.

- Key design decisions (KDDs) are documented after careful consideration of available options for enabling such capabilities.

- They are assessed for an impact across various areas such as process, configuration, data, and so on.

- New SAP S/4HANA capabilities are then finalized, and decisions related to customizations and RICEFWs are made.

Additional References

- https://help.sap.com/doc/f45c88b65643403d976824 84273216d0/1809.000/en-US/SIMPL_OP1809.pdf

- https://rapid.sap.com/bp/#/browse/categories/ sap_s%254hana/areas/on-premise/packageversions/ BP_OP_ENTPR

- https://help.sap.com/viewer/product/SAP_ READINESS_CHECK/200/en-US

CHAPTER 4

Development in S/4HANA

Development in SAP S/4HANA is very much dependent on the implementation approach you choose. The development approach and tool set differ whether you are going for Greenfield implementation or Brownfield implementation.

Although we outline the key differences, we are not jumping into the nitty gritty of development coding and methods of configuring tools, as you can always refer to the links provided in the Appendix or SAP Developer Network (SDN) blogs for step-by-step instructions. The focus of this chapter is highlighting how the SAP S/4HANA development approach differs from the earlier versions of SAP and introducing you to the development tools available.

Initial Considerations

If you are already a developer working in the SAP ERP environment, you already know how crucial it is to be familiar with the list of tables in each process area and the relationships among them. Prior SAP database architecture followed the principle of replication of business documents and associated data structures. It led to complicated database relationships with a slew of tables representing a single process area.

© Sanket Kulkarni 2019
S. Kulkarni, *Implementing SAP S/4HANA*, https://doi.org/10.1007/978-1-4842-4520-0_4

For example, you have business documents such as sales order forms, purchase orders, invoices, and so on. An early data decision was to design database tables exactly mirroring the information to be stored in them. As is normal for database tables, each of these tables had its primary key with added dimensions such as quantity, location, currency, and so on.

Over time these tables ballooned into monolith structures with status fields, aggregates, headers, and line item tables with very intricate relationships between them. What would happen, for example, if you changed a quantity in the sales order form? All associated tables then had to duplicate all other fields and update the change log accordingly. This led to an exponential increase in the size of database tables. If you are a developer, you can understand the pain of developing a report in such a complicated table structure.

First, you had to understand all those relationships and then develop a report by intelligent use of indexes and header and line item relations. Performance was a real concern, as you need to fetch data from all these table structures before you can generate insightful data. Second, consistency of data had to be maintained across the board, causing serious table locking issues. If you were updating the status field in the header table, the associated item status also had to be updated. Such duplicity among queries and updates led to a lot of performance implications. As a developer, you also had to consider the performance implications of any slight change you made to a program. This would result in anxiety during upgrades or patches and often required extensive testing every time you made a change.

Development in the earlier SAP ERP environment was a slow, waterfall-based process, working around this spider web of tables. Most custom logic resided in the application layer with occasional database layer modifications. It was therefore based on a classical approach for custom development, which is to calculate on the application layer and minimize database calls from performance and locking considerations.

With SAP S/4HANA, SAP has tried to address these problems with traditional development. Here are the critical changes in SAP S/4HANA that directly affect development.

- New code line with Columnar HANA Database

  - SAP has completely rewritten the code line to fit the in-memory columnar HANA database structure. Unlike the clear segregation of business logic at the application layer, now logic resides not just in the application layers, but also at the database layer. It is feasible to do this in SAP S/4HANA because the columnar structure in HANA DB allows for multiple program calls without incurring any performance issues.

  - Another reason for SAP opting for more a straightforward code line is the readiness for multitenant, cloud-based ERP, as it would have been a nightmare to convert the traditional relational database into the multitenancy feature required by the cloud-based ERP.

- Large database tables instead of many interlinked small tables

  - The HANA table structure consists of large database tables with 200 to 400 fields representing single business documents entirely. The concept of the header table and associated item tables is thus now redundant.

  - Although conceptually all your business documents are still stored in the large database tables with 200 to 400 fields, every field acts as an index key.

> So what happens if you change the quantity in the sales order form document? Only the specific field representing quantity gets updated, and all other fields remain unchanged. The benefit of this approach is a reduced HANA database size, as there is no replication of entries for every small change.

- Locking or performance issues do not occur as database changes are swift and small.

- No aggregation of entries

  - With the HANA database, there is no need to aggregate or store aggregated data separately in associated tables. The SAP program can read all the records in the master table faster and generate aggregates on the fly.

  - There is also no need for separate status tables at each header or item level, due to faster access, as the index is on every field in the table.

- Due to the elimination of the need to develop and maintain separate indexes on the database table, the work required of developers, as well as database administrators, is also significantly reduced. The index is at each field level in the HANA Database table.

Due to the simplification of table structures, development has also become a lot simpler in SAP S/4HANA. The development approach is also changed to move calculations to the database layer and use an application layer for transferring results. This results in the benefit of reduced testing and maintenance effort.

Development effort during SAP S/4HANA implementation is driven by a combination of two factors.

- Implementation approach
  - Greenfield implementation focuses on the development of objects from scratch, with limited reuse of developments in the existing ERP system. Development guidelines are defined up front. A majority of the effort is spent on the development and testing of new RICEFW objects.
  - Brownfield implementation focuses on the migration of development objects from the existing SAP instance. Thus significant development effort is spent on remediation of objects because of database and code line changes.
- SAP S/4HANA edition
  - The On-Premise Editions follow native SAP S/4HANA development guidelines.
  - The Cloud Editions follow the extensibility framework guidelines based on the SAP Cloud Platform.

Whereas Greenfield implementation can potentially use development guidelines applicable to the On-Premise or Cloud SAP S/4HANA editions, Brownfield implementation follows native SAP S/4HANA development guidelines as relevant to the On-Premise Edition.

Greenfield Implementation

Greenfield implementation is an implementation of SAP S/4HANA from scratch. Depending on the SAP S/4HANA edition—On-Premise or Cloud—development guidelines (also called the extensibility framework) change.

The On-Premise Edition has a choice of either native SAP S/4HANA development or SAP Cloud Platform. Cloud Editions solely use SAP Cloud Platform for their development needs.

Native SAP S/4HANA Development

As shown in Figure 4-1, there are multiple scenarios for native SAP S/4HANA development. You can use native development to build integration with SaaS applications like SAP Concur, SuccessFactors, and so on, using prebuilt content. You can also use it to make extensions like additional fields and reports. Custom Fiori apps or analytical apps using Core Data Services (CDS) also follow the native SAP S/4HANA development approach using development tools like HANA Studio. More details are provided in Chapters 9 and 10 regarding custom Fiori apps or CDS views.

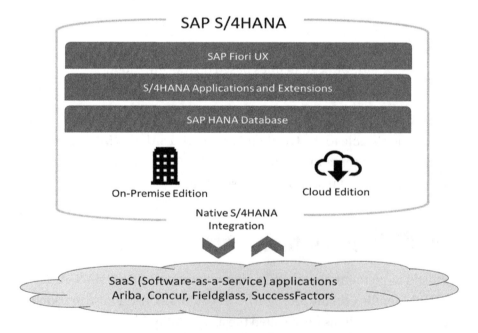

Figure 4-1. *Native SAP S/4HANA development architecture*

You should opt for native SAP S/4HANA development –under these conditions.

- You are looking for on-point extensions such as adding or updating fields in HANA DB or applications, developing custom forms, or making minor changes in the UI.

- You want to apply specific business rules and logic locally.

- You want custom reports and analytics internal to your organization with customizations in CDS views.

- You want a classic, in-app extension (also called Fiori extensions) based on Unicode or SAP HANA enabled code development.

SAP Cloud Platform

SAP S/4HANA is not just an ERP solution, but also a full-scale digital platform on which intelligent applications can be built. Development for such applications is done in a cloud-native format so that it is applicable not just for the cloud apps interacting with on-premise SAP S/4HANA applications, but also for native apps in cloud applications.

SAP Cloud Platform is a platform-as-a-service (PaaS) used to connect both on-premise and cloud-based SAP S/4HANA or other third-party software. It uses open standards like Java, JavaScript, Node.js, and Cloud Foundry for development.

As compared to native SAP S/4HANA development with limited capabilities, SAP Cloud Platform offers a more diverse range of services across various categories, some of which are listed here.

- Runtimes and containers with virtual machines

  - Java

  - XSJS (SAP HANA extended application services, classic model JavaScript)

  - HTML

  - Cloud Foundry Services

- Data and storage

  - SAP Cloud Platform Big Data services

  - SAP Cloud Platform SAP HANA service

  - SAP Cloud Platform Document service

- DevOps

  - Continuous Integration and Continuous Delivery

  - SAP Cloud Platform Web integrated development environment (IDE)

  - SAP Monitoring Service

  - SAP Translation Hub

- Integration

  - SAP Cloud Platform Integration

  - SAP Cloud Platform Remote Data Sync

  - SAP Agile Data Preparation

  - SAP Cloud Platform OData Provisioning

  - SAP Cloud Platform API[23] Management

  - SAP Cloud Platform Workflow/Business Rules/Connector

- User experience

    - SAP Fiori Cloud

    - SAP Cloud Platform Portal

    - SAP Cloud Platform Forms by Adobe

- Mobile

    - Mobile Service for development and operations

    - Mobile Service for app and device management

    - Mobile Service for app protection

    - Mobile Service for SAP Fiori

    - SAP Cloud Platform SDK for iOS

- Analytics

    - SAP Cloud Platform Predictive Services

    - SAP HANA for Advanced Analytics

    - SAP BusinessObjects Cloud[24]

    - SAP Leonardo

- SAP Cloud Platform Internet of Things

- Security

    - Cloud App Security with SAP Cloud Platform

    - SAP Cloud Platform Identity Authentication + Provisioning

As evident from the functionalities listed, cloud-native development for SAP S/4HANA has many considerations as compared to native SAP S/4HANA development. It involves several intricate steps, from managing code bases, injecting library dependencies, and configuring system properties, to production deployment at scale.

Such services can be broadly categorized as follows.

- Infrastructure-as-a-service (IaaS), which provides virtualized computing resources in the SAP HANA infrastructure over the Internet.

- PaaS, which provides shared application services and capabilities required for the development of new multitenant cloud applications or extensions of existing solutions residing either in on-premise or cloud environments.

- SaaS, which offers software licensing and delivery models on a subscription basis.

Here are a few of the principles that drive the design of SAP Cloud Platform–based applications.

- APIs

  - They abstract an application from the underlying technology implementations. APIs should be designed in such a way that they address a complete and straightforward use case.

  - Each API implements a specific function and does not rely on other API calls within the application.

  - For example, a sales order status query application might use functions such as authorization, data verification, and ATP information. Each of these functionalities is designed as a separate reusable API function.

- Error handling

  - Errors in the distributed environment should not affect user experience and should not interrupt the service. An API service is designed to address failures from other API functions either by continuing the process unaffected or presenting failure information to the user. In planning, you specifically look at such failure points in the process and develop necessary failover mechanisms.

- Authorizations

  - Security is needed in every layer of the application: cloud computing environment, secure coding, and access control inside an application. Proper authorization mechanisms should be developed at each stage of the process.

- Distributed environment

  - In a distributed environment, components of an application leverage API services dynamically. Such application components are designed to operate independently in a distributed environment.

- Performance

  - You should design an application for optimal performance (on clearly defined performance benchmarks). End-to-end performance is dependent on the performance of the end user as well as the back end.

  - The performance of an end user depends on the network latency. *Network latency* is the term used to indicate any delay that happens in data communication over a network. You should design the application based on the different latencies available to the end users.

- Performance of a back-end application (e.g., SAP HANA back-end views in the case of SAP S/4HANA On-Premise Edition) depends on several data requests sent. An optimized number of requests to retrieve data helps fine-tune the performance.

One of the primary advantages of using SAP Cloud Platform are the many folds started for having a managed platform, so no additional effort is required for upgrades and operations to the built-in security, scalability, and easier integrations. The SAP Cloud Platform also provides development tools such as the S/4HANA Cloud Extension SDK and Web services for integration with the SAP S/4HANA Cloud Edition. You should use SAP Cloud Platform in the following circumstances.

- You get inputs from external devices or users in the process (e.g., IOT sensors sending equipment data for monitoring).

- You integrate with SAP cloud apps (e.g., Ariba, Concur, SuccessFactors) as well as non-SAP SaaS or cloud solutions. There is native integration with SAP cloud apps as well.

- Your processes cross boundaries between on-premise and cloud apps, and thus need cloud connectors to provide a seamless experience to the users.

- You are developing stand-alone apps using partner assets in advanced technology applications (e.g., machine learning, automation, blockchain, etc.).

- You want to decouple a system of record (back-end SAP ERP) at the same time you require reliable data and process integration.

- You want to have mobile–cloud integrations and significant UI adaptations like mobile and tablet user experience for your customer portal.

Brownfield Implementation

Brownfield implementation involves conversion and migration from an existing SAP ERP system (ECC or SOH) to an SAP S/4HANA instance.

Development in Brownfield implementations is mainly focused on addressing the impact of HANA DB migration and new code line in SAP S/4HANA on your custom code elements such as function groups, programs, and class objects. Although the actual fix can be swift and in most cases minor, it is essential to conduct a detailed impact analysis up front and determine a plan of action. Such a custom code impact assessment helps to address the following concerns.

- Which parts of your custom code must be changed to avoid potential functional issues?

- Which parts of the custom code should be optimized to achieve the same performance with SAP S/4HANA as earlier?

- Will the custom code lead to different results after migration due to column-based storage and changes in the table structures?

Once identified, changes in your custom inventory can be categorized as follows:

- *Necessary changes:* Most of these may have already been covered via SPAU/SPDD transactions. Transaction SPDD allows you to adjust modifications to ABAP Dictionary objects during the conversion and Transaction SPAU allows you to adjust programs, function modules, screens, interfaces, documentation, and text elements. If you use hard-coding, practice of presetting values directly in the program or extensively referred custom tables during customizations, such changes are marked as 'Necessary' changes.

- *Application-level optimization:* Due to a change in the development approach (shifting work from the application layer to the database layer), application-level changes can be redesigned with specific considerations about performance benchmarks.

- *Database migration adaptations:* Doing away with status and aggregate tables in SAP S/4HANA has considerably improved performance even for custom programs. Such changes should be evaluated up front against existing performance benchmarks. If you are referring to existing indexes (SAP standard or the ones set by the database administrator [DBA] team), your custom code might need to be adjusted accordingly.

Using Code Inspector

SAP provides a tool called Code Inspector, which gives you first-level analysis in terms of the extent of the changes required to your custom code. This tool runs your custom code inventory against the SAP S/4HANA simplification list.

Here are the different checks conducted by SAP Code Inspector.

- The Search DB Operations check

    - It checks for the write operations on specific database tables.

- It checks whether your custom code uses DB-specific features like native SQL and DB hints.

- It checks whether code relies on implicit sorting of database queries or performs operations on physical pool or cluster database tables.

- It checks whether it uses function modules to retrieve technical DB index information.

- The Field Extension check

  - It finds length conflicts in your coding for material number fields.

- The Search for usages of simplified objects

  - It finds usages of objects against the ones stored in the simplification list.

- The Search for ABAP dictionary enhancements

  - It checks the usage of append structures, DB views, and customizing tables as mentioned in the simplification database.

- The Search for simplified DB tables, which are used as base tables in custom DB views

- S/4HANA-related syntax errors fixed via SAP notes mentioned in simplification items

Further detailed line-by-line analysis should also be done by your development team against each error reported by the SAP Code Inspector. Each error reported is then identified with the following details, for necessary correction.

- Line number.

- Error description.

- Actual field used.

- Join conditions between tables.

- Where condition was used.

- Internal table details.

At the end of the custom code impact assessment, you will have a clear idea about affected programs and fixes as needed (mandatory, application level, database level).

Because not all programs are going to be used once you migrate to SAP S/4HANA, you should identify the programs to be fixed as first priority and the ones that can be discarded after due consideration. This also gives you a fair idea in terms of what code can be pushed to the database level instead of an application level.

Apart from the custom code inventory, there are also going to be new RICEFWs due to new functionalities you want to introduce or new Fiori custom apps you wish to enable. Treatment of new RICEFWs works the same way as in a Greenfield implementation. As stated earlier, you have the option of either native SAP S/4HANA development or SAP Cloud Platform.

Custom Code Remediation

The process for custom code remediation during Brownfield conversion of an SAP S/4HANA implementation is as follows.

1. You start with an SAP S/4HANA Readiness Check, which is a filter on the Simplification List for SAP S/4HANA (as discussed in Chapter 3) based on usage of your existing SAP ERP system. The SAP S/4HANA Readiness Check performs a remote analysis of the settings, configuration, transactional data, and transactions and reports used in the production system (or a recent

copy of production); derives the functional usage of the system; and then lists all simplification items relevant for this system. It also provides the following details:

- Minimum system and landscape requirements (Unicode + AS ABAP as mandatory) along with version interoperability for peripheral systems such as SAP PI, BW, APO, Fiori, and so on.

- Incompatible business functions that will be switched on during the conversion.

- Incompatible SAP add-ons.

- BW extractors that will work or will not work, along with potential remediation for the same.

- Custom code evaluation in terms of HANA compatibility, access to obsolete tables (INSERT, UPDATE, DELETE, MODIFY), and custom code dependent on deprecated or changed components.

2. Custom code impact assessment is done using SAP Code Inspector.

3. Obsolete objects are removed from the list of affected objects. Outdated code, unnecessary modifications, and clones are removed from the system.

4. On identification of the affected objects along with the degree of impact, prioritization of fixes is done. Based on the preference, the following custom code adjustments are made:

- Adjustment starts with applying modification using SPDD and SPAU due to software update.

- Then mandatory changes are performed for SAP HANA if the system is not on SAP HANA already. A few examples of such changes are listed here:

  - If code relies on implicit sorting, adjustments are necessary because there is no implicit sorting by primary key in SELECT statements without ORDER BY in HANA DB.

  - Compatibility views redirect SELECT statements for the obsolete tables automatically to the new tables. Adjustments for the SELECT statements are made if needed.

  - INSERT, UPDATE, MODIFY, and DELETE statements are rewritten for references to obsolete or changed tables in custom code.

  - Custom DDIC views on top of the obsolete tables are replaced with open-SQL SELECT statements. DDIC views are application-dependent views that combines data from several existing tables.

  - Custom fields in obsolete tables are transferred if they do not exist in any other table.

5. There are functional changes to be made to the custom code inventory due to SAP S/4HANA data model changes as follows:

   - *Material master:* Extension of field length of the material master from 18 to 40 characters.

   - *SD/MM:* New table PRCD_ELEMENTS for storing document conditions, with an extended field length of several fields and other changes.

- *SD:* Simplified Order Management, a merge of status information into document or item tables (from the dedicated table) and elimination of status tables, simplification of the document flow table, removal of indexes for sales documents, and elimination of rebate index table VBOX.

- *MM:* Simplified Inventory Management, material document table MADOC replacing the existing material document, elimination of aggregates and history tables for stock quantities, inventory valuation via Material Ledger only.

- *FICO:* Universal Journal, Unified Financial document table ACDOCA ("Universal Journal") replacing multiple line item tables across G/L, CO, AA, ML; elimination of aggregates and indexes.

Note   SAP has released notes with step-by-step instructions on custom code remediation for each of these functionality changes. Please refer to them during the implementation.

---

6. Next, check whether the remediated custom code meets the same performance benchmarks as used in the earlier SAP ERP system. You can follow these guidelines to make sure that performance does not deteriorate any further:

   a. Keep the result sets small.

   b. Minimize the amount of transferred data.

   c. Minimize the number of data transfers. Use array operations for INSERT, UPDATE, and DELETE when changing many records. Avoid nested SELECT loops.

    d. Minimize the search overhead.

    e. Keep data-intensive calculations away from the database.

7. Finally, custom code is also checked for Unicode compliance if the source SAP ERP is not yet on Unicode.

In general, your existing custom code should run as before, after the process of remediation. If your custom code is too reliant on your old SAP ERP database (indexes, custom tables, etc.) or accesses cluster tables where data from multiple tables is stored, then the remediation process becomes essential.

The testing effort is also directly proportional to the changes in custom code inventory. You should thoroughly test each change you make to the custom code as part of the remediation process. The testing process should check the functionality, but also performance. If your code is going to affect the interfaces, then make sure that you run the end-to-end scenario instead.

Additional References

- https://blogs.sap.com/2017/02/15/sap-s4hana-system-conversion-custom-code-adaptation-process/

- https://blogs.sap.com/2016/09/12/s4hana-extensibility-use-case-overview/

- https://blogs.sap.com/2017/09/07/extensibility-highlights-of-s4hana-cloud-1708/

- https://blogs.sap.com/2017/09/15/get-started-with-your-sap-s4hana-cloud-side-by-side-extensions-in-5-simple-steps/

- https://scn.sap.com/docs/DOC-46714

- https://help.sap.com/doc/9dcbc5e47ba54a5cbb509afaa49dd5a1/201809.002/en-US/CustomCodeMigration_OP1809.pdf

CHAPTER 5

Data Conversion in S/4HANA

Data conversion is an essential part of your SAP S/4HANA project. If you opt for a Greenfield implementation, data conversion means the extraction, transformation, and loading of your legacy data into SAP S/4HANA. If you opt for a Brownfield migration, then the data conversion process is much simpler, as you need to migrate data from the source SAP ERP system to SAP S/4HANA. SAP provides tools to automate the entire data conversion process in this case. Thus, the data conversion process is executed much faster. More details on the data migration process and associated tools can be found in Chapter 7.

Let us now discuss various aspects of data conversion as executed during SAP S/4HANA implementation.

Phases of Data Conversion

Data conversion consists of three main phases: extraction, transformation, and load.

- Extraction

  - During the extraction phase, data is pulled from one or many of the existing legacy systems. In some cases, it will be manually constructed.

  - This process is done via extraction programs built on the legacy side.

- Transformation

  - During the transformation phase, the extracted data is altered into the format expected by SAP S/4HANA.

  - Automated mapping rules are developed to adapt extracted data to the SAP S/4HANA format.

  - Additional data quality checks are done as part of the transformation process.

- Load

  - Data is loaded via automated programs or by individual records manually by an end user into SAP S/4HANA.

  - Manual data load is done where the number of records is minimal, and the development of load tools is too complicated and costly.

Data conversion discussion starts early during an SAP S/4HANA project. During the planning and assessment phase, you start with defining your business data requirements. During the design phase, you detail data design considerations as follows.

- Data objects in scope.

- The subset of the data to be converted.

- Mandatory and optional fields for a data object.

- Business rules for each field and object.

- Validation of values for each field.

- Security classification as per General Data Protection Regulation (GDPR) or similar regulations.

During the build phase, several mapping rules are configured, and load programs are developed. During the test phase, multiple cycles of mock conversions are executed to fine-tune the data conversion process further. Once it is optimized in terms of performance as well as runtimes, final data conversion is performed during the cutover and deployment phase.

Your data conversion strategy for SAP S/4HANA should cover all four of these aspects:

- Data objects in scope.

- Tool sets.

  - Should cover mechanisms for data extraction, profiling, transformation, and loading.

  - Automated vs. manual loading.

- Data conversion processes.

  - Key steps involved, including dependencies among them.

  - Mock conversion and dress rehearsal process.

  - Data validation, before loading data and once it is loaded successfully.

  - Data profiling and cleansing activities.

- Organization.

  - Who owns the data?

  - Who is responsible for data quality?

  - Who does data cleansing and validation?

Data Objects in Scope

Each data object is categorized as one of the following:

- Master data

  - It consists of the data objects with longer a life cycle and is used repeatedly in business transactions.

  - For example, customer master describes an entity with which you do business. Once created, it gets updated only when there are changes to the customer's information (address, phone number). This customer record can be used in a variety of business documents such as sales orders, contracts, and invoices.

- Transactional data

  - It represents transactions that take place in the SAP S/4HANA system. It is very dynamic and references one or more master data objects.

  - Examples include sales orders and purchase orders.

During the design phase, the inventory of data objects is finalized. This drives all further discussions on transformation and loading processes. Once completed, specific field-level requirements are defined in the detailed design phase.

Another important consideration developing a security classification for data conversion objects based on GDPR or similar regulations. Such classification drives specific data to be scrambled in nonproduction for privacy concerns, often best done at the source during the extraction process. Masking or encrypting data early ensures proper security throughout the conversion process from the source systems to the SAP S/4HANA deployment.

Please note that for data conversion during SAP S/4HANA deployments in Europe, the GDPR must be considered. The GDPR (EU Regulation 2016/679) is a regulation by which the European Parliament, the European Council, and the European Commission intend to strengthen and unify data protection for individuals within the European Union (EU). It also addresses the export of personal data outside the EU. The regulation was adopted on April 27, 2016 and applied from May 25, 2018. More details can be found at `https://en.wikipedia.org/wiki/General_Data_Protection_Regulation`.

Table 5-1 provides the representative list of data objects used during the SAP S/4HANA implementation.

Table 5-1. *Data Objects Used During SAP S/4HANA Implementation*

Area	Master Data	Transaction Data
Common	Financial Master	
	GL Accounts–Global/ Company Code	
	Profit Center	
	Cost Center	
	Supplier Master (Business Partner–Supplier)	
	Customer Master (Business Partner–Customer)	
	Material Master	

(*continued*)

Table 5-1. (*continued*)

Area	Master Data	Transaction Data
Finance	Bank Keys	GL–Balances
	Exchange Rate	GL–Open Items
	Asset Master	AP–Open Items
	Activity Type	AR–Open Items
	Activity Price	
	Assets Values	
	Condition Contract	
Procurement	Purchasing Info Record	Purchase
	Purchasing Category	Orders–Open
	Quota Arrangement	Items
Manufacturing	Characteristic	Process
	Class	Order–Open
	Bill of Material	Items
	Work Center–Resources	Stock Balance
	Recipe	
	Production Route	
	Production Version	
	Inspection Characteristic	
	Inspection Plan	
	Inspection Task List	
	Inspection Lot	
Sales and	Customer-Material Info Record	Sales
Distribution	Pricing Condition	Order–Open
	Output Condition	Items
	Route Determination	
	Material Determination	
	Contract for Pricing	

Data Conversion Tool Sets

SAP provides a variety of tools to extract, transform, and load data into SAP S/4HANA.

SAP Data Services and Rapid Data Migration

SAP recommends SAP Data Services (DS) and Rapid Data Migration (RDM) as the primary data conversion tool for SAP S/4HANA. SAP provides the basic SAP DS with S/4HANA. If you need any additional data quality tools with specific functionalities for data deduplication, data parsing, or geolocation matching, and so on, they can also be added to the package.

RDM provides about 50 prebuilt standard SAP S/4HANA master and transaction data objects. The RDM package covers the entire process of data conversion, including extract, transform, cleanse, map, and upload to SAP S/4HANA.

Once the RDM package is configured, you can execute the following steps to accelerate data conversion for specific objects.

- Connect to legacy data.

- Map legacy data to SAP S/4HANA structures.

- Execute an object processing job and complete the extraction process.

- Validate extracted data in terms of data quality (consistency, uniqueness, and Completeness).

- Map input values to SAP S/4HANA data structures.

- Load data into SAP S/4HANA.

- Validate data into SAP S/4HANA.

Table 5-2 lists the various prebuilt RDM packages available for SAP S/4HANA data objects. New objects that are not part of RDM can be built directly in SAP DS.

63

Table 5-2. Prebuilt RDM Packages

Batch	Routing
Maintenance Plan	SD Pricing
Production Order	Inventory Balances
Secondary Cost Element	Functional Location
Characteristic	Cost Center Groups
Class	Source List
Activity Type	Work Breakdown Structure
Activity Price	Fixed Assets
Exchange Rate	Purchase Info Record
Cost Centres	Planned Independent Requirements
Profit Centres	Order Reservations
Bank Master	Purchasing Requisition
Customer Master	Contracts
Vendor Master	Scheduling Agreements
Work Centre	Sales Order
Material Master	Purchase Order
Material Master Classification	Internal Order
Configuration Profile for Material	Open Deliveries
Inspection Method	Activity Type Groups
Material Inspection Type	Profit Centre Groups
Material Inspection Characteristics	Business Partner (Customer and Vendor)
Inspection Plan	Statistical Key Figures
Bill of Materials	Supplier Invoice
Equipments	Credit Memo
Service Master	Data Migration Data Quality
Object Dependency	Customer Invoice Billing
Material Customer Replenishment	
Reference Operation Sets	

Along with SAP Data Services, you can also consider using SAP Information Steward (IS), a data quality profiling and monitoring tool. With SAP IS, it is possible to build data quality rules based on the business rules provided in the data mapping documents and verify the data quality during the mock conversions or final load.

There are various data quality capabilities useful during data conversion, including the following:

- Matching scoring.

- Consolidation.

- Standardization.

- Parsing.

- Cleansing.

- Geocoding.

SAP IS also provides multiple dashboards to measure data quality through the different data quality dimensions, capture score trends, drill down to a field level.

SAP Legacy System Migration Workbench

Use of SAP Legacy System Migration Workbench (LSMW) is not recommended for SAP S/4HANA. However, it is still used as a backup plan when some objects do not work correctly in SAP DS or other methods.

Migration Cockpit and Migration Object Modeler

Migration Cockpit (MC) is built using SAP Landscape Transformation (SLT) technology. It was originally built to support extract, transform, and Load (ETL) for SAP S/4HANA in the cloud, so their functionalities are simpler and easier to use because the cloud version of SAP S/4HANA is simpler than the on-premise version.

Migration Object Modeler (MOM) is a functionality built into SAP S/4HANA to support modifications and updates to the standard programs and data models prebuilt in MC.

Figure 5-1 provides an overview of the data conversion process and tools to be used during SAP S/4HANA implementations.

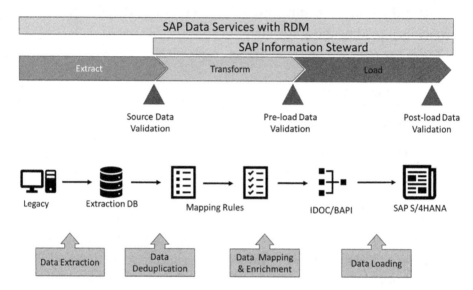

Figure 5-1. *S/4HANA data conversion process with tools*

Data Conversion Methods

There are two ways in which data conversion happens during SAP S/4HANA implementation: automated or manual. The automated method uses programs and tools to extract data from the legacy source systems, transform it, and then load it into SAP S/4HANA. It requires the programs to be designed, coded, and tested with end-to-end automation.

It is useful with the following conditions:

- A large number of data objects in scope for conversion.

- Large volumes of records and fields for most data objects.

- Complex cleansing and transformation rules.

- Limited cutover window, the time frame to extract, transform, and load all data objects.

- To mitigate the risk of human error during manual steps.

- Repeatable data conversion process to execute multiple mocks and cutover.

The manual data conversion process is used when a data object has a small volume of records and fields. Data is manually entered into the SAP S/4HANA system using specific transactions (t-codes). A manual load is also considered when the amount of data manipulation is excessive for the automated approach. Manual conversion requires no development effort and is very flexible. However, this approach should be avoided due to the high chance of human error and time constraints.

Particular objects and source systems will require manual steps and manual loading due to technical limitations. The threshold for manual loads is often based on the volume of records, several columns, and complexity of data, typically capped at 100 records.

Some organizations prefer to develop a hybrid approach, which is a combination of the manual and automated methods. It has an automated process with limited manual intervention, to ensure that the conversion and validation process is successfully executed, repeatedly practiced, and then delivered during cutover. Such a semiautomated approach is used where the data is manually collected or constructed in data load template files, but automatically loaded via a loading tool.

Data Conversion Processes

In this section, we discuss key data conversion processes followed during the SAP S/4HANA implementation.

Data Cleansing

Data cleansing focuses on the quality of data. It involves analyzing data, identifying inaccuracies, and making the necessary corrections to data. Data profiling acts as input to the data cleansing exercise. Data cleansing is run throughout the SAP S/4HANA implementation to ensure data quality improves over time.

The source of the data is the legacy system from which its extracted. Data cleansing is focused on the extracted data for further analysis. It checks current data against (1) standard SAP field rules, and (2) business rules as defined by the process teams. Such an exercise, when automated, is referred to as *data profiling*. The results of profiling provide insight into the current quality of the data and the amount of effort required to update values as per the requirements of the SAP S/4HANA system. The data profiling exercise assesses extracted data across these parameters:

- Uniqueness to ensure data records with their attributes are not duplicated.

- Completeness to ensure all mandatory data is filled.

- Accuracy to validate appropriate values are populated.

- Integrity to ensure data is correctly referenced to drop-down values.

- Conformity to confirm proper formatting of data in terms of field lengths and data types.

The data profiling reports help you discover quality issues and generate recommendations for data cleansing.

Corrective action is taken either by manually correcting data or automated uploading in the source system. Corrections happen in the legacy system before the extraction. The direct manual method is preferred to address obvious data quality issues, like misspelled names, incorrect or incomplete addresses, and so on. It is also used in cases when work cannot be completed programmatically and requires manual intervention.

On the other hand, automated uploading helps you update multiple records at once; for example, status fields. It is used when many documents need to be updated using similar values. If not available, you will need to develop such a mass update tool in the legacy system.

In some cases, you cleanse the data within a tool like SAP Data Services instead of in the legacy system. It is suited to cleansing activities where precise rules can be defined to enable a systematic addition, update, or replacement of values; for example, mandatory fields expected by the SAP S/4HANA data structure. In such a case, source data in the legacy system is still inaccurate, although the load files for each mock and final load contain the correct values.

Data cleansing done in the SAP Data Services tool falls under data transformation activity. There are various ways in which data transformation is achieved during SAP S/4HANA implementation.

- Relevancy rules determine the relevance of the extracted data by performing cross-checks between master and transactional data. Such rules separate the live data from data that is obsolete. For example, you might decide to deactivate a particular plant. Master and transaction data related to that inactive plant is filtered out. Only current data is then sent to SAP S/4HANA.

- Data standardization ensures the data is in in the same format and fields as required by SAP S/4HANA. It is performed by checking addresses, postal codes, and country codes against third-party data.

- Data deduplication is done by identifying and analyzing duplicate master data records.

  - Matching criteria are applied to enable the identification of duplicate records. For example, the same name, address, postal code, and city might help you identify duplicate customer master records.

  - Such records are presented to the user, who identifies unique records and tags the rest of them as duplicates. Such duplicate records are filtered out, and individual records are sent to SAP S/4HANA.

  - You also develop a deliberate mechanism to systematically deactivate duplicate records and delete associated transaction data so that such records do not appear in further iterations.

- Data enrichment is done by mapping legacy values into target values relevant for SAP S/4HANA. For example, plant 1234 in the legacy system is mapped to PL01 in the SAP S/4HANA system. It also involves filling in the missing (but mandatory) information before data loading.

Data Validation

Data validation is a process of validating the converted data based on specific criteria during the ETL process. There are two ways in which data validation is done.

- Systematic data validation is done by the data conversion teams and process teams. It is achieved by using conversion reconciliation tools to reconcile the data throughout the conversion process.

- Business data validation is done by business data object owners who own the converted data. It is achieved by having business resources verifying the SAP S/4HANA screen values with data load files.

  - Because manual verification of data takes quite an effort, you might decide to validate only the sample data size of the total converted records. If its small-sized data consists of up to 100 records, you might check the entire set of records one by one.

  - You can do manual data validation either by count matching, aggregate validation, or spot checking for data in the legacy and SAP S/4HANA system.

Data validation is typically performed at three points during the entire ETL cycle.

Postextraction Data Validation

In this activity, the extracted data is validated to match the selection criteria and relevancy rules defined for the extraction process. This ensures that only the intended set of records is extracted.

Posttransformation Data Validation

In this activity, transformed data is validated once transformation rules are applied before loading into the SAP S/4HANA system. You compare the final load file against the data transformation rules (including data mapping rules) and ensure all the transformation logic is correctly applied to the data.

Postload Data Validation

Once the data load is completed, a comparison is made between the load file and the SAP S/4HANA data to ensure that the data is loaded correctly and ready to be used in business transactions in the new system. Note that once data validation fails at any step, corrective action should be taken. Data should be reloaded and validated again to ensure identified issues are sorted out, and data quality is up to par.

Not all data validations are necessary for all converted data objects. Business data validation is needed to validate data when it is extracted, transformed, and loaded using a tool. Manually constructed data might need only postload validation. Because you manually prepare the data, no transformation logic is applied to it. Therefore, it is assumed that the data is accurate and complete as is. On the other hand, data objects with currency values or calculations might need all three types of validations. Data objects with low complexity and low volume only need posttransformation and postload validation.

Mock Data Conversion

Mock data conversions are the test cycles where the end-to-end data conversion process and tools are tested and continuously refined for all data objects. For each mock conversion, you set up activities and the scope of each data conversion cycle (ETL). Depending on the data scope, you could decide to run as many mocks as needed.

Mock data conversion testing often precedes with test cycles such as system integration testing, performance testing, and user acceptance testing. A portion of the converted data from the mocks is used as test data for these test cycles.

- Before the start of each mock conversion cycle, the following prerequisites should be in place.

  - A mock conversion plan, including the detailed steps and timing for the conversion of data from the source systems to SAP S/4HANA. This includes extraction, transformation, load, and validation timelines.

  - Mock environments with adequate sizing specifications to prevent impact on the processing time of the data conversion programs.

  - Proper access for the data conversion team as well as the data validation and cleansing team.

  - Completed functional configuration in the SAP S/4HANA system as per the requirements of data objects.

  - Data conversion tools required to execute the mock built and unit tested. By the time the final mock is performed, you should have all data conversion tools in place.

  - Data validation scripts prepared with step-by-step instructions that business data object owners follow during each data validation.

- The following details are tracked during each mock cycle for every data object.

  - Processing time for extraction, transformation, load, and validation and cleansing.

  - Record counts.

  - Load results.

- Initial mocks might include the limited set of data, depending on the readiness of data objects in terms of extraction programs, transformation rules, and load programs. They are used to validate dependencies between various data objects and to test the sequencing of data conversion activities.

  - Subsequent mocks are run with a full set of data to be used for various test cycles and help refine the end-to-end data conversion cycle, including sequencing of data objects and runtimes. As execution times are recorded with each data conversion step, incremental data load happens with each iteration until the production-size data load is executed successfully.

  - Data validation, as well as cleansing, is completed to ensure proper data quality.

  - The final cutover and data deployment plan with the necessary tasks, timings, sequence, and resources (both local and remote resources) is confirmed based on the results of the final' production size load. This mock test cycle (often called dress rehearsal) ensures that 100% of master and transaction data is successfully loaded within the designated time.

Data Conversion Cutover

Data conversion cutover is the set of data conversion activities performed to transition from the legacy system(s) to the new SAP S/4HANA system. The activities are like those executed during a mock conversion cycle, except that data load is directly done into the production system during a small window of time. The final cutover and data deployment plan with the necessary tasks, timings, sequence, and resources is followed closely as each step is executed in sequence by the respective teams.

Data conversion activities at cutover start with an initial load of master data once all the prerequisites for data readiness are met. Transaction and historical data load are followed by systematic and business data validation of the cutover loads. If any errors are encountered, they are fixed either manually or programmatically. Data is reloaded or set directly into the production system. Once business data object owners validate and sign off on the data load, data conversion cutover is complete.

Data Freeze

Before data conversion cutover, data creation and maintenance activities in the legacy systems are halted for a specific period. This process is called the *data freeze.* The purpose of the data freeze is to extract all relevant data from the legacy systems and load it into SAP S/4HANA without risk of the data being changed. If such changes continue to occur in master and transaction data in the legacy system, it causes issues related to data consistency in SAP S/4HANA. For example, change in the material attributes or open order items causes problems among the business users doing the postload validation and might require extensive analysis to identify and fix discrepant data. Reloading of such data in the production environment might cause additional issues unless tested thoroughly in the lower environments.

In cases where data freeze cannot be planned, dual maintenance forms are maintained. These are the templates populated manually by business users to record data additions, updates, and transactions. These updates are then keyed manually into the SAP S/4HANA system after data conversion cutover is complete. Such dual maintenance adds a lot of effort for tracking and then syncing with SAP S/4HANA, so it's often done only for a limited period.

Business Partner Data Conversion

With SAP S/4HANA, customer and vendor masters are redundant. Instead, the approach now is of a Business Partner, which is a universal account that could play multiple roles within the organization.

The specific tables for customer data (KNA1) and vendor data (LFA1) remain available and are not affected. Although it is a good idea to keep business partner ID and customer ID and vendor ID the same, it might not be possible in the case of overlapping number ranges. Here are some of the options in case of overlapping number ranges between partner IDs.

- You can choose to the harmonize vendor and customer master. For example, you can retain the customer number range while the vendor number range is migrated to the customer number range. Then, business partner IDs are generated from the same number range.

  - The problem with this approach is that you lose the history of your vendors, as the vendor data is divided over two numbers.

  - During data conversion, specific mapping rules are to be developed to map old vendor numbers to new business partner IDs.

- You can choose to keep the same vendor and customer IDs and link them to the business partner with a whole new number range.

    - You do not lose the history of your vendors and customers. Also, you do not have to expend additional data conversion effort to map them to the new number range.

    - It does not affect external integrations with third parties that use current customer and vendor numbers.

- You can choose a hybrid approach, which is a combination of the preceding strategies, based on the different number ranges allocated to the specific types of vendors and customers.

Additional Reference

- https://blogs.sap.com/2017/05/29/migrating-data-to-your-new-sap-s4hana/

CHAPTER 6

Testing Effort in S/4HANA

Testing plays a significant role in SAP S/4HANA. Although the testing approach might differ based on the implementation approach—Greenfield or Brownfield—you should give testing due consideration in the various testing cycles involved. The primary objective of testing in SAP S/4HANA should be to ensure there is no negative impact to current system design and performance.

Testing Considerations

Here are a few reasons why testing for SAP S/4HANA is unique as compared to any ERP-based transformations.

- SAP Fiori provides an entirely new approach in the SAP user experience (UX), in terms of dashboards and apps. It means that testing should be done for functionality as well as performance, for each FIORI app you enable.

- The SAP HANA database provides a simplified table structure and ease of access as well as development. Migration from any database (from your source ERP) to

© Sanket Kulkarni 2019
S. Kulkarni, *Implementing SAP S/4HANA*, https://doi.org/10.1007/978-1-4842-4520-0_6

HANA results in a change of standard as well as custom code. All custom code changes should be in your test scope and thoroughly tested.

- Data migration and conversion play an important role regardless of the implementation approach. Because a large amount of data gets migrated to SAP S/4HANA, performance issues are bound to occur. Unless you give specific attention to testing, especially mock conversion and a dress rehearsal, it will cause problems later.

- Interfaces are not expected to change a lot due to backward compatibility proposed by SAP. Still, you should assess and individually test each one of them end-to-end to make sure that they work as before.

All of these reasons warrant a deliberate testing approach. Such a test approach is developed as early as the planning phase and covers a wide range of test cycles such as regression testing, functional unit testing, performance testing, and system integration testing.

Note that based on the industry you are in, there will be additional testing considerations. For example, the pharmaceutical industry will need to execute other performance qualification (PQ), operational qualification (OQ), and infrastructure qualification (IQ) testing as part of validated testing.

Testing in SAP S/4HANA also differs in the way it executes during various phases of the project. Testing execution starts early in SAP S/4HANA. It is advisable to execute a full regression test up front as part of the planning and analyzing phase. This helps to determine the impact on the current business processes. Such inputs can help process teams to finalize process-level customizations and affect further test scope.

In addition to the regression test being executed up front, you should run a performance test well before the planned testing activities. SAP S/4HANA involves extensive technical changes in the underlying table structures that have a direct impact on the execution of job performance and efficiency. Understanding these impacts before the design phase is crucial in minimizing the risk to the overall performance of your SAP S/4HANA system. During the design and build phases, you conduct functional unit testing as well as assembly testing. Unit testing involves detailed testing of a configuration or development object to ensure that any programmable logic or functionality is thoroughly tested. In the case of any custom code remediations, it includes testing specifically for logic as well as error processing. You should also test performance-related fixes if there are any. Assembly testing, on the other hand, tests the entire business scenario associated with program fixes and customization. In case of the interfaces, it includes testing an end-to-end scenario right from the trigger to the receipt and acknowledgment mechanisms.

Once your solution is tested in the development environment, you can transport it to a production-sized test environment and retest it. This test ensures that any functional and performance issues are identified during the build phase itself.

During the test phase, you conduct a full-scale integration testing, which includes several test cycles. Each test cycle could consist of iterations of midmonth and month-end closing processes. Apart from that, you should conduct necessary performance, regression, and dress rehearsal testing as well, including the following elements:

- Custom objects (RICEFWs), both newly developed and remediated, as in the case of Brownfield implementations.

- Process-level configurations and customization. Even if you are opting for best practices, it should be part of the test scope.

- Add-on and third-party applications.

- User profiles and authorizations.

- Conversion processes and timing.

- Performance and stress service-level agreements (SLAs).

- Data archival testing.

- Automated and background jobs.

- Interfaces, both inbound and outbound.

- Data conversion and migration process (mocks).

- HA/DR SLAs.

S/4HANA Test Environments

SAP S/4HANA testing will be comprised of several environments to execute all the test components. Depending on your SAP S/4HANA landscape and overall complexity of the transformation (driven by the level of customization and scope), you will need to provision new production-size environments for testing. It is prudent to run performance tests in such production-size environments. Dress rehearsal testing (to finalize the data conversion template), as well as day-in-the-life testing, is also done in such production-size environments. There might be new environments to simulate HA/DR scenarios.

As you can see, the test approach drives the choice of environments. Within each test environment, instances and clients for each test are also identified. You should have a specific strategy to control and manage changes and transports throughout these systems. For the long-planned SAP S/4HANA program, there might also be a parallel source SAP ERP environment. Retrofits from source SAP ERP are released to such environments via specific transport management layer. Managing retrofits from source SAP ERP on top of native SAP S/4HANA changes can be difficult and should be monitored closely.

The environment strategy should ensure data integrity and consistency across all test environments because it needs to support multiple test cycles of your SAP S/4HANA implementation being executed in parallel.

S/4HANA Test Cycles

Testing in SAP S/4HANA proceeds through a variety of test cycles. Each test cycle then goes through a series of iterations until the defect level is within the acceptable limit.

As part of the test strategy, for each test cycle, you define the following:

- Test objectives, by explaining the purpose of the testing.

- Test scope in terms of scenarios and customizations.

- Test entrance criteria and prerequisites.

- Test exit criteria for sign-offs.

Test entrance criteria consist of the following:

- Test environments with relevant test data in place, based on the test cycle. For example, if you are running the performance testing cycle, you will need production-like test data.

- The documented defect management process.

- Established test execution and management tool sets like HP ALM.

- Detailed test scripts and scenarios.

Test exit criteria can include the following:

- A log of test script execution in the tool.

- A record of defects found, fixed, and retested.

- A log of open issues, root cause analysis (RCA), and associated remediations.

- Test results signed off by the process lead or owner.

Let us discuss various test cycles executed during SAP S/4HANA implementation.

Functional Unit Testing and Assembly Testing

Functional unit testing is conducted in several cycles, in Agile iterative fashion. At the end of each sprint or release, a group of functionalities is thoroughly tested in the development environment for logic as well as performance. Native error processing is a focus of such testing. For example, if you are testing a sales order creation scenario, you explicitly check for missing or incorrect information (e.g., inappropriate material and sales organization association) and check whether a program can catch and intimate the user as expected.

You also transport related objects to a test environment with a production copy of data and run additional tests there. The objective is to get early indicators pertaining to the impacts of the changes, in terms of end-to-end business scenarios as well as performance. Called an assembly test, this is conducted in multiple cycles during SAP S/4HANA implementation. Such due diligence is necessary, as many cross-functional changes happen during the execution and potentially affect the month-end closing process and interfacing applications.

First test passes might include new and remediated RICEFWs as well as configuration items. During later passes, you run full month-end closing process, including running prerequisite steps. Such a testing process allows unit as well as assembly testing of your customizations and helps you assess the impact on the month-end closing process.

Key objectives of functional unit testing and assembly testing are as follows:

- To conduct frequent functional testing of the customization objects after a build cycle in a production-like environment.

- To finalize the new month-end closing process based on the customizations.

- To assess the impact of downstream applications and plan for remediation before system integration testing.

System Integration Testing

System integration testing (SIT) consists of end-to-end testing of the business processes. It is executed in iterative mode, with relevant data sets loaded on demand. Mock conversions with production data copies are loaded before each test pass. Each test scenario could cover multiple customizations embedded in the business process and aims to test all aspects, including Fiori apps.

For example, a sales order processing scenario might cover specific interfaces from Customer Portal or Hybris. It could also include any customizations done in the SAP UX, namely Fiori. It can even extend to Embedded Analytics and analytical apps related to sales order tracking. Such a test scenario in SIT includes execution of a series of test cases, with data flowing from one test case to another. Multiple passes result from intermittent failures of test steps and subsequent fixing efforts.

SIT is also essential from an interfaces perspective, as you can also test remediations on legacy systems to ensure that they can receive and send data appropriately. It is a test of interoperability between SAP S/4HANA and peripheral systems in terms of handshakes and data transfer so that business processes are executed seamlessly and consistently.

It succeeds in assembly testing. Because its focus to test end-to-end workings of the business process, it might not test full functionalities of each customization while the month-end closing process is retested to reaffirm the significant steps and outcomes. You should also include a year-end closing process once the month-end closing processes are tested successfully.

Apart from testing all customizations (referred to as development RICEFWs and configurations), you should also test the following:

- Reporting if you have EDW like SAP BW.

- Embedded Analytics for real-time reporting and dashboards.

- SAP UX developments including Fiori apps.

- User profiles and authorizations.

The key objectives of SIT are as follows:

- To ensure that the SAP S/4HANA system, data, and processes meet the business requirements.

- To simulate business operations.

- To ensure upstream and downstream applications interface seamlessly.

User Acceptance Testing

User acceptance testing (UAT) provides an opportunity for superusers to test critical business scenarios, including interfaces, and assures that the SAP S/4HANA solution satisfies essential business requirements.

The challenge in executing UAT is to identify proper representation in terms of stakeholders. If you are rolling out an SAP S/4HANA solution in multiple geographical and business units, you should make sure that all key stakeholders are part of the UAT cycles. Although it is done centrally, it is also essential to run UAT from a subset of locations to check connectivity and local infrastructure. Such localized UAT cycles also help validate user experience from end-user sites; for example, how FIORI apps fare in terms of functionality and performance.

If you are rolling SAP S/4HANA out to multiple locations, language considerations might apply. They influence SAP UX (including FIORI apps) as well as Adobe interactive forms developed in ABAP. Because not all FIORI apps support multilingual capability, this presents a further complication. It means that UAT test scenarios should clearly highlight such exceptions and individually test with target (multilingual) user groups.

Infrastructure, including printers, should be set for UAT in a production-like environment. Sometimes the user will need to print forms or labels at local printers, and UAT allows you to test such scenarios.

The test scope for UAT should also represent enough day-in-the-life scenarios to be relevant for end users. For example, as a purchasing planner, the user might be expected to use a Fiori dashboard to review open items, run MRP (Materials Requirement Planning), and review purchase requisitions in specific FIORI app. Using a standard set of data to run day-in-the-life scenarios is a good idea, as you can refer to the same document numbers throughout the test case and get a clear understanding of how the end-to-end business scenario works.

You should use adequately masked production data for testing instead of dummy data. Because production data is loaded into the UAT environment, associated data conversion testing is also done.

Dress rehearsal testing is run in parallel with UAT to ensure mock data conversion works with production-size data within the stipulated time. It also makes available enough data to run UAT scenarios as UAT is executed in production-like environments. You can also identify any gaps in the design and build phase and plan mitigation for it. The purpose should not be to expand the scope, but instead to identify gaps for the deferred action.

The following are the key objectives of UAT.

- To validate the SAP S/4HANA solution against the business requirements.

- To confirm that the solution supports the business processes and is accepted by the business users.

- To highlight any gaps in process design and plan mitigation.

It is important to note that UAT should not result in scope expansion for your SAP S/4HANA program.

Performance Testing

Performance testing is done during SAP S/4HANA implementation to ensure the capacity of the system to handle peak capacity requirements. This SAP S/4HANA system capacity is measured in these two ways:

- The number of users simultaneously logged into the system.

- The volume of data being transferred or processed at once.

Because the technical architecture supports peak capacity requirements, a sizing exercise becomes crucial. Performance testing is done by simulating production-like systems. Testing includes running end-to-end business processes across applications with high transaction volumes. System response times are monitored closely.

If you are already running enterprise-scale ERP, you might already have performance benchmarks for specific transactions and batch jobs. While migrating to SAP S/4HANA, performance testing ensures that these specific response times, or performance benchmarks, are met.

There are multiple passes of performance test execution throughout the life cycle of the project. Performance testing begins much earlier due to the expected impact of the SAP S/4HANA migration to job performance. Due to the underlying database-level changes, it is crucial to evaluate performance-wise impact on the business processes. You should run a performance test at the beginning of the design phase for essential business processes, regardless of whether you use SAP best practices or not. The results of this initial performance test allow you to identify objects for performance optimization.

Subsequent passes of performance testing include a variety of tests. The load test is the test where simultaneous access by multiple users is simulated and response times to log in and execute key transactions are captured. The stress test simulates commonly used transactions for access by an incremental number of users until it breaks. This helps you understand peak user capacity of the system. An endurance test simulates larger volumes of data transfer and replication or big batch jobs over time while average user transactions are processed. This helps you understand the impact of large-scale data replications in terms of routine operations over time. Another variation is called a peak test, where you expose the SAP S/4HANA system to peak capacity (say multiple users are accessing at once) with regular loads in parallel like ongoing batch jobs and data transfer. This simulates the real-life environment and assesses the impact on the existing architecture. A throttle test is used in the case of Fiori apps and Customer Portal, where limited virtual users access the SAP S/4HANA system from outside the organization via multiple channels or devices. Response time for such users is measured to make necessary performance optimizations.

Here are some of the criteria that will help you identify candidates for performance testing.

- High-risk, large-volume transactions; for example, planning runs, and data replication via interfaces such as SLT, BODS, and CIF (Core Interface) for SAP APO.

- Critical month-end and year-end closing processes.

- Large-volume deployment tasks such as customer–vendor integration.

- Data ETL programs dealing with large volume objects like material masters and business partners.

- Critical custom programs with known performance issues.

- Key business transactions with higher user volumes; for example, sales order processing.

- Process chains for extraction to SAP BW/EDW.

- Critical interfaces dealing with a large amount of data in real time; for example, MDG (Master Data Governance) and Central Finance.

These are some of the key objectives of performance testing.

- To run specific end-to-end volume test cases for critical business flows.

- To simulate batch and online transactions and capture response times in line with the given benchmarks.

- To identify system bottlenecks and generate performance tuning recommendations to optimize response times.

Regression Testing

Regression testing is done during the early stages of SAP S/4HANA migration. It is especially relevant if you are undergoing Brownfield migration.

You run regression tests in the test environment with a copy of production data along with all the latest changes from the production environment retrofitted for SAP S/4HANA if required.

If you already have regression test scripts from the source SAP ERP, you can use them with minimal modification. Ideally, your regression test scenario should include complete month-end closing (all SAP standard and custom processes and a subset of interfaces with downstream applications).

Issues identified during regression testing are the direct input to the analysis phase. Such an inventory of affected objects helps shortlist objects for remediation. Because you will have many more issues than regular regression tests running in the source ERP, you should expect longer runtimes than usual.

Another scenario where regression testing will help is retrofits. Treatment of retrofits during the project is a complicated topic, as projects go live at different times as compared to SAP S/4HANA conversion timelines. Because changes need to be in sync with the SAP S/4HANA environment, they are brought over by the retrofit mechanism (merely copying and pasting the code unless you have a transport management layer in place). Limited regression testing is recommended in this case to make sure that such changes do not negatively affect existing functionality in the system.

The key objectives of regression testing are as follows:

- To get a complete list of affected objects as an input into the planning and analysis phase.

- To test all standard and custom objects including a full month-end closing process.

Data Conversion Testing

Data conversions (called mocks) help with data migration to production as well as nonproduction environments. Data conversion testing is done by performing several practice runs in a test environment with production-size data. They are synchronized with various test cycles that use production data for testing. Mock conversions are run before SIT and performance testing.

Data conversion testing involves validation of the following items.

- Proper sequencing of automated and manual conversion activities, including runtimes taken by each step.

- The readiness of data conversion tools and programs; for example, BODS, LSMW, and Microsoft Excel templates.

- Simulation of production volumes and their impact on the conversion runtime.

Executed before cutover, data conversion testing (also called dress rehearsal) ensures the readiness of data conversion at go-live time. The final data conversion schedule is arrived at based on results from earlier mock conversions as well as the dress rehearsal. Such a plan will provide information about data objects, the order in which they will load (dependencies), and the timing of how long each will take in a production environment.

The following are the key objectives of data conversion testing.

- To rehearse and refine the go-live data conversion plan, including sequence, dependencies, duration, resources, and so on.

- To validate data conversion programs and manual conversion procedures.

- To simulate data cleansing, validation, and reconciliation processes.

Security Testing

Security testing in SAP S/4HANA is done once the development of security roles is completed in the build cycle. It is done through both positive and negative testing. Positive testing ensures that you have access for the transactions used in the authorization profile assigned. Negative testing ensures that you do not have access for transactions not in the authorization profile.

Security testing is done in three stages.

- Unit testing is done to verify a single transaction can be executed. This identifies and remediates the errors in security roles in the early stages and confirms all transactions in a security role can be accomplished.

- Integration testing is done to assess the functionality of the security role(s) assigned to the business role. It is designed to test the integrity of the business role so that improper business functions cannot be executed in the system.

- UAT is performed by business users who will be mapped to their approved business roles to verify a subset of business processes.

Defect Management Process

You should implement a proper defect management process during SAP S/4HANA testing, as you will execute a variety of testing during the project. Different types of defects (e.g., performance vs. functional) are discovered and thus should be appropriately categorized.

The defect management process involves three steps.

- Identification is where you will create a defect by documenting the problem and initiating an investigation into why a test condition or step in a test script did not execute as expected.

- The investigation is where you will analyze the issue and develop solutions

- Resolution is where you will fix the problem and retest. Every decision will not necessarily lead to program changes. Some might lead to a change in business practices, as well. Once retested successfully, the final decision might be configuration change, a business process change, a technical fix, a bug being reported to SAP, or even a design change.

As part of the defect management process, you also develop defect classification based on the criticality level, which helps you prioritize defect resolutions. Critical or high-priority defects are aggressively fixed and are monitored closely as go/no-go criteria for the go-live launch. Lower priority defects can be candidates for workarounds and added to the backlog eventually.

CHAPTER 7

Technical Architecture Effort in S/4HANA

Technical architecture considerations for SAP S/4HANA are far different than traditional on-premise ERP systems. The SAP S/4HANA stack is very much focused on the future, suited mainly for the digital transformation of your business. Technical architecture discussions in SAP S/4HANA implementation revolve around three aspects.

- Infrastructure aspects
  - Can SAP S/4HANA and the associated SAP stack be hosted on the cloud?
  - What are S/4HANA versions are best suited from an infrastructure perspective? Should you use the On-Premise Edition or Cloud Edition?
  - What are the storage and performance considerations?
    - With an optimized database, your storage considerations are going to be reduced compared with traditional ERP. Sizing helps you arrive at the appropriate number.

© Sanket Kulkarni 2019
S. Kulkarni, *Implementing SAP S/4HANA*, https://doi.org/10.1007/978-1-4842-4520-0_7

- You would like similar or better performance than traditional ERP provides. What are new performance benchmarks, considering SAP UI will move to Fiori?

- Migration aspects

  - You can implement SAP S/4HANA in three different ways. The choice of an implementation approach also affects the way you will migrate data to SAP S/4HANA.

    - Greenfield implementation.

    - Brownfield implementation.

    - Staged Brownfield (also called Bluefield) implementation.

  - SAP provides various tools to support S/4HANA installation and migration, depending on the implementation approach. You need to determine which tool is appropriate for your approach.

- Security aspects

  - With Fiori, internal as well as external parties can access the SAP S/4HANA system. What are the security aspects for mobility and the Fiori UI, and in general for SAP S/4HANA?

High-Level Architecture

Let us first understand the high-level technical architecture of SAP S/4HANA. As seen in Figure 7-1, S/4HANA resides on the back-end SAP HANA database. The application layer in the middle is often called the

S/4HANA core access database tables via CDS views. Transactional logic as well as logic for analytics functionalities (covered in Chapter 10) often resides the in S/4HANA core.

Please note that business logic resides in both the S/4HANA core as well as the HANA DB level, for faster reporting and retrieval. The SAP Gateway connects the SAP UX layer, including Fiori, to the S/4HANA core.

The end user accesses the SAP UX layer via SAP Web Dispatcher, which is responsible for routing user requests to the S/4HANA stack.

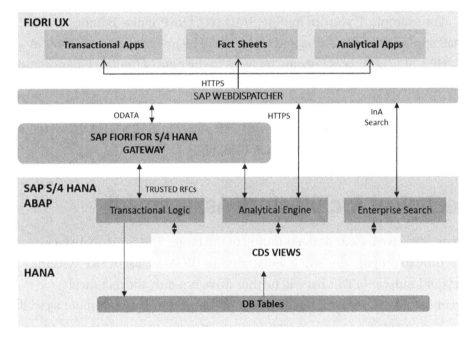

Figure 7-1. *S/4HANA architecture*

Please note that Figure 7-1 does not cover associated on-premise as well as cloud-based SaaS components that might be present in your SAP landscape. Apart from non-SAP legacy systems, you might have separate instances for other SAP systems such as SAP APO or CRM. Such systems will be integrated to target the SAP S/4HANA instance eventually.

SAP provides a set of tools to integrate the SAP S/4HANA On-Premise and Cloud editions with legacy applications that are not part of the SAP S/4HANA suite. SAP HANA Cloud Integration (HCI) is the preferred process integration middleware. Tools like SAP Landscape Transformation Replication Server (SLT) and SAP Enterprise Information Management (EIM) also facilitate data transfer. SLT is often used for real-time data replication sourcing from SAP ERP or non-SAP systems into S/4HANA, as in the case of Central Finance. EIM refers to the tools like IS and the Data Services platform, as well as PowerDesigner.

For example, if you opt for SAP S/4HANA On-Premise Edition, all SAP SaaS applications like Ariba and Concur will be integrated into S/4HANA via HCI. SLT/EIM tools become relevant in the case of Central Finance and MDG implementations.

Your technical architecture considerations for SAP S/4HANA should include such integration aspects with SAP and non-SAP S/4HANA systems along with necessary tool sets (HCI, EIM, SLT).

Technical Architecture Assessment

Once you have a clear understanding of the target SAP S/4HANA stack, it is time to prepare the SAP bill of materials (BOM), a list of SAP systems in your landscape. This list will further drive not only the technical architecture discussions, but also licensing and cloud procurement as well.

You can start a technical architecture assessment once you have the final SAP BOM. You will do it during the early days of the SAP S/4HANA project, in conjunction with the planning phase.

- Technical architecture assessment decides on various important topics such as datacenter strategy.

    - Where are your primary and secondary (backup) datacenters located?

    - What is your HA/DR strategy?

- What is the availability SLA for datacenters?

- Scalability requirements

  - What are your sizing requirements in terms of storage and performance?

  - Which environments are hosted on the cloud? Is it going to a public or private cloud instance? How are cloud virtual machines (VMs) provisioned: on-demand or fixed capacity?

  - Are there any security requirements?

  - Are there any data privacy requirements (e.g., GDPR)?

- Change management landscape

  - What is my SAP deployment landscape? Does a three-system landscape—Development ➤ Quality ➤ Production—suffice, or do I need a more complex one?

  - If you are running an SAP ECC/ERP production instance in parallel while SAP S/4HANA goes live, what is your retrofit strategy? How will changes in the SAP ECC/ERP system flow to SAP S/4HANA during the project life cycle?

Datacenter Strategy

Datacenter strategy revolves around careful evaluation of your HA/DR and backup and restore processes. You might need to provision additional hardware capacity for proper failover and restore functions with defined availability SLAs, define node and site failover, and appropriately restore capabilities.

Suppose you have two datacenters—let us call them DC1 (primary) and DC2 (secondary)—along a with remote datacenter. Your datacenter strategy will revolve around synchronous replication between DC1 and DC2 and asynchronous replication to the remote datacenter.

In such a case, you have two alternatives:

- Combined HA/DR protection within DC1 and DC2.

- Storage system only in highly protected DC2.

Such an arrangement makes sure that there is no data loss when a link to DC1 is lost. It also reduces the probability of data loss in the case of disaster with DC2. That way, you have local failover within the datacenters for hardware and software failures. The application server and SAP hardware in DC2 can also be used for nonproduction systems.

In summary, your datacenter strategy for SAP S/4HANA will be dependent on the choice of infrastructure (DC network).

- For low-latency, stable inter-DC network:

  - Host-auto failover with synchronous storage replication.

  - Host-auto failover with synchronous system replication.

- For the limited interDC network:

  - Host-auto failover with backup and log shipping.

Scalability Requirements

Scalability and performance constitute a big consideration for your SAP S/4HANA project. It is not only driven by simple memory and storage considerations, but also by performance considerations. There are three scenarios in which you can run S/4HANA sizing with the QuickSizer tool.

- Greenfield S/4HANA sizing.

- Sizing based on the existing SAP ERP system.

- Sizing based on existing SAP system working on HANA Database.

You can also add specific performance benchmarks as part of the sizing exercise. Here are some examples.

- Can SAP S/4HANA process more than 3 million orders in less than two hours?

- How can I consolidate five functional ERP systems into one?

- How can I migrate 10 TB of SAP ECC data to S/4HANA?

Note that translating business requirements into sizing requirements is an iterative process and thus needs to consider a variety of angles, including commercial considerations. For example, you can also look at business growth, mergers in the pipeline, or large functional extensions from a sizing perspective. Such business parameters might or might not affect all sizing components. Clarity on the impact of respective factors on sizing components is important and drives sizing decisions.

For example, you are experiencing substantial business growth and would like to know how it affects SAP S/4HANA sizing. A simple table, like the example shown in Table 7-1, will provide clarity on the impact on sizing decisions.

Table 7-1. *Example Sizing Evaluation Table*

S/4HANA Sizing Component	Affected by Business Growth
Operating system	No
HANA caches/services	No
HANA working memory	Yes, indirectly
Business data (Columnar Store)	Yes
Metadata (Row Store)	Partially, if growth affects DDIC entries in the metadata

The output of the sizing exercise is the capacity recommendations for PRD (Production) and non-PRD (non-Production) S/4HANA landscape, in terms of memory size, disk size, and CPU (related to memory).

Change Management Landscape

Change management landscape covers the SAP S/4HANA production as well as nonproduction landscape. You will also consider the PRD and non-PRD landscape, including software change management and non-PRD sizing.

After the sizing assessment, you evaluate various deployment models; for example, you might opt for standard deployment for production and virtualized deployment for nonproduction systems. Table 7-2 illustrates a variety of S/4HANA landscapes. Note that variations might exist owing to the specific considerations of retrofits or coexistence of production and project environments, for example. Industry considerations can also drive the choice of the landscape; for example, the pharmaceutical industry will need a computer system validated environment for testing and production.

Table 7-2. *S/4HANA Landscapes*

Landscape	Description	Environments
3-system landscape	Applicable for moderately customized S/4HANA implementations	Development ➤ Quality ➤ Production
4-system landscape	Applicable where additional test cycles are needed; for example, validated testing in the pharmaceutical industry, or performance testing in high-data volume environments	Development ➤ Quality ➤Testing ➤ Production
5-system landscape	Applicable where production and project track run in parallel; for example, you have already gone live with pilot site and then rolling S/4HANA solution in other sites	Development 1➤ Quality 1 ➤ Production Development 2➤ Quality 2

The higher the number of customizations while implementing SAP S/4HANA, the more complex your SAP landscape will be. You will need to test more, expend more effort during deployment, and devote more time to support as well.

S/4HANA Migration

There are three different ways in which you can implement SAP S/4HANA. Your choice of implementation approach affects technical architecture decisions such as tools to be used and steps to be followed for conversion. Please note that I am using terms such as conversion and migration interchangeably. In principle, it means the transfer of data and customizations from the source SAP ERP to the target SAP S/4HANA version.

- Greenfield implementation

    - It involves the plain "vanilla" installation of S/4HANA on a hosted environment.

    - Data migration is done using tools such as Data Services. You create customization from scratch or manually lift-and-shift from the source ERP system in specific cases. Refer to Chapter 5 for more details on data migration for Greenfield implementation.

- Brownfield Implementation

    - It involves the plain "vanilla" installation of S/4HANA on a hosted environment.

    - Data, as well as customizations, are migrated using a set of tools provided by SAP.

- Staged Brownfield (Bluefield) implementation

    - This relatively new approach is a variant of a Brownfield implementation where you migrate customizations up front and migrate data in batches.

    - It is suitable for scenarios where you are deploying SAP S/4HANA in stages; for example, across regions in multiyear rollout programs.

Because the technical architecture plays a major role in SAP S/4HANA conversion during Brownfield implementation, we discuss only the key aspects in this chapter. Please note that I have skipped most of the technical details, as you should refer to the respective SAP guides for step-by-step implementation.

Step 1: Establish Prerequisites

This step makes sure that all of the following preconditions for installing SAP S/4HANA are met.

- The source SAP ERP must be a Unicode-enabled system. SAP does not support Unicode conversion during the migration to SAP S/4HANA. If your SAP ERP is not Unicode-enabled, it should be enabled first, then migrated to SAP S/4HANA. This is often called a two-step process. If your ERP is an older SAP Business Suite release, you should upgrade it to SAP ERP 6.0 EHPxx first before considering migration.

- Migration to SAP S/4HANA does not require source SAP ERP already on HANA DB. SAP Migration tools take care of any DB to HANA DB conversion.

- Migration can happen only from ABAP Stack Application Server. Your SAP Application Server might be dual stack (ABAP as well as Java Stack). Some organizations favor a dual-stack approach where they can do any process customization on ABAP, and the Java stack is used as a wrapper for using SAP NetWeaver components like Portal/ITS. You should split a dual-stack architecture before you go ahead with SAP S/4HANA migration.

- If you are already using Fiori, and thus have a Fiori front-end/gateway server, it should be connected by the new SAP S/4HANA system via a hub-deployment model. Existing Fiori apps will continue to run as if they are connected to the older back-end system. For the connection to the S/4HANA back end, the Fiori Apps should be redeployed and configured.

Step 2: Prepare for S/4HANA

This step involves multiple checks to be run in conjunction to assess S/4HANA migration impact and take corrective actions if needed. Maintenance Planner is used to check the following components.

- Any add-ons to your system.

- Any active business functions in your system. Note that if you have a certain business function in an always-on state in the source SAP ERP that is to always be off in SAP S/4HANA, it causes a potential conflict during migration.

- Industry solutions.

Maintenance Planner can flag such components for attention if it finds that there is no valid conversion path for them. If the Maintenance Planner check is successful, it generates the files necessary to download (add-ons, packages, and the stack configuration file) for migration. Key information is populated in the stack configuration file (stack.xml) to be used by Software Update Manager (SUM), a tool responsible for SAP S/4HANA migration.

An SAP readiness check for SAP S/4HANA is run to check several aspects related to SAP S/4HANA implementation. The precheck tool validates installed software components and checks functional requirements as well as usage of business functions. The simplification database checks the impact on the custom code by simplification items.

As covered in Chapter 4, custom code changes in a Brownfield implementation are not just related to database (as in from any DB to HANA), but also related to the functionality as well as a performance optimization.

With the simplification of the SAP standard code, a lot of standard objects were modified, joined, or decommissioned. They have a direct impact on the custom code, relying on SAP standard objects. This analysis calls out each SAP standard object that could have an impact on the custom code, often referred to as simplification items.

You can use either of the following tools during SAP S/4HANA migration.

- The simplification item list is a PDF document that describes the change and the expected impact for each simplification item.

- The simplification item database is a tool-based analysis approach that compares the actual simplification item list with the source ERP system based on an extract of the custom code metadata.

Beside of the adjustment of the custom code to meet the simplification item requirements, there is still the need to ensure that the custom code is running functionally correct on an SAP HANA DB. SAP tools present the analysis in the following four main categories:

- Mandatory changes to ensure functional correctness.

- ABAP-based changes to ensure no performance degradation.

- ABAP-based changes for performance optimization.

- DB-based development (code push down) for performance optimization.

Please note that it is good practice to adjust all DB independent mandatory changes in the source system to reduce the effort required and duration for the migration project. You can also run usage analysis in the source SAP system to pinpoint frequently used custom objects and fix them specifically for SAP S/4HANA migration. That way, the effort needed for custom code remediation is optimized.

Step 3: Complete SAP S/4HANA Migration

This step starts with the activation and deactivation of business functions identified in Step 1. You execute the functional prerequisites in terms of necessary add-ons and industry solutions. The

The stack file (prepared by Maintenance Planner) is now ready to be used by SUM. The SUM tool starts by cleaning up noncompatible add-ons or any third-party tools. Then, it begins the installation of SAP S/4HANA and then executes the Database Migration Option (DMO) to migrate the necessary configuration as well as data to the new SAP S/4HANA instance.

Please note that you have other advanced options to migrate data and configurations to SAP S/4HANA. A few of them are listed here. You can check for further details in relevant SAP documents.

- *SAP DMO:* SAP direct migration to HANA (combining migration with upgrade).

- *SAP Downtime Optimized DMO:* Migrating specific application tables during uptime to minimize downtime.

- *SAP Near-Zero Downtime (NZD):* Minimizing downtime for business-critical environments.

- *SAP Landscape Virtualization Management (LVM):* Automate post copy and migration steps.

You should also check whether there are any follow-on activities for specific functions, for example, finance. Finally, you should do custom code remediation by implementing any mandatory changes (database as well as functional), followed by rigorous testing (functional unit testing). Further, you have to adjust the custom code related to simplification item lists and test it thoroughly.

Once completed, you have a fully migrated SAP S/4HANA instance for Brownfield implementation. Please note that the impact on existing interfaces by SAP S/4HANA migration is minimized by SAP ensuring backward compatibility with the data model on traditional databases. It should therefore not affect all the interfaces, but it would make sense to test all interfaces during SIT.

S/4HANA Migration in Four-Tier Landscape

Suppose your source SAP ERP is on a four-tier landscape, such as Sandbox ➤ Development ➤ Quality ➤ Production. If you want to migrate to a four-tier SAP S/4HANA landscape, you should execute the following steps.

1. Start by preparing the SAP ERP sandbox system as a copy of the production system.

2. Run Maintenance Planner, prechecks, and custom code checks in the Sandbox system of the source SAP ERP. Maintenance Planner will subsequently create a stack file based on the analysis.

3. Run SUM data migration, along with a software update, in the Sandbox system. Follow-on activities for Finance are complete. Perform custom code remediations (SPAU/SPDD) along with any delta changes. The SAP S/4HANA Sandbox system is ready for use now.

   • The purpose of this exercise is to establish the steps and time taken for SAP S/4HANA migration.

   • It also highlights any issues like data inconsistency or business function conflicts up front.

4. Set the SAP ERP development system to Code Freeze, which means no further changes are allowed until migration. Execute Maintenance Planner, prechecks, and custom code checks, and generate a stack file for the development system.

5. Execute SUM data migration, along with a software update, in the development system. Follow-on activities for Finance are complete. Perform custom code remediations (SPAU/SPDD) along with any delta changes. The development system is ready with steps and time taken for SAP S/4HANA migration validated.

6. Refresh the SAP ERP quality system with production data. Execute Maintenance Planner and prechecks. Note that the quality system will also have a similar Code Freeze restriction during migration. Then, generate the associated stack file.

7. Execute SUM data migration, along with a software update, in the quality system. Follow-on activities for Finance are complete.

8. Import transport requests related to custom code remediations (SPAU/SPDD) along with any delta changes, into the quality system. Now, your quality system is ready with steps and time taken for SAP S/4HANA migration validated.

9. Execute Maintenance Planner and prechecks in the production environment and generate a stack file.

10. Execute SUM data migration, along with a software update, in the production system. Follow-on activities for Finance are complete. You import transport requests related to custom code remediations (SPAU/SPDD) along with any delta changes, into the production system.

11. Finally, your SAP S/4HANA production system is ready with complete configuration and data migrated successfully.

Security

The objective of SAP security is to protect the SAP S/4HANA installation by maintaining its confidentiality, integrity, and availability. The guiding principle of SAP S/4HANA authorizations is that every user should have access only to the information and resources that are necessary for a legitimate purpose. You grant only the privileges that are essential to do the user's work within SAP S/4HANA. Often termed *least privilege,* this is a principle-based approach, not an absolute rule. There will be instances where the benefits of applying the least privilege principle will not outweigh the risks of granting additional access privileges.

The SAP S4 HANA authorization concept involves the assignment of general as well as detailed user authorizations to the user master. These assignments can reach down to the transaction, field, and field value levels. Actions by a user might require several authorizations. For example, to change a material master record, authorizations are required for the following:

- Transaction "change."

- Specific material type.

- Views of the material master record.

- General authorization to work with the company code.

Such authorization requirements often require deliberate effort from SAP security teams to build a complex relationship between authorization objects and fields, often called building blocks for SAP security design. Figure 7-2 shows the hierarchical relationship between various aspects of SAP security design.

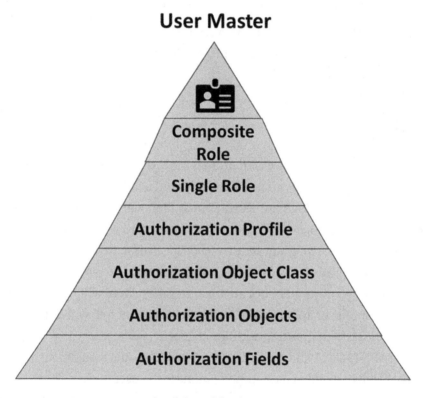

Figure 7-2. *SAP security building blocks*

- *Authorization field:* This is the smallest unit against which you do the authorization checks. The fields in an authorization object contain permissible values in specific data elements. During authorization checks, SAP validates such values against the input. If satisfied, then access is given only to the user.

- *Authorization object:* An authorization object groups all related authorization fields necessary for authorization. All the fields are checked simultaneously for user access.

- *Authorization object class:* This is where you combine authorization objects into logical groupings of authorization objects.

- *Authorization* is the authority to perform an action in the SAP system based on a set of authorization field values in an authorization object or class. Each authorization refers to exactly one authorization object and one or more possible values for each authorization field listed for that authorization object.

- *Authorization profile:* This contains authorizations for different authorization objects. User authorizations are assigned using authorization profiles.

- *Single role:* A role is a set of functions or transactions describing activities done by the user.

- *Composite role:* Also known as a collective role, this is a group of several different (single) roles. Note that composite roles themselves do not contain authorization data. If an authorization change is required in a composite role, the authorization data must be maintained in the (single) roles.

SAP Security Design and Build

As part of the SAP S/4HANA implementation, you design the security roles in a manner that supports compliance objectives of your organization. Security role design should be efficient to maintain and enable the least privilege principle stated earlier. The SAP Profile Generator (PFCG) is used to create roles and generate profiles. With the Profile Generator, you define the roles for various job functions, with allowed activities. It then serves as a link between the user and the corresponding authorizations. The Global Role transaction requirements are used as the basis to build all the end-user roles. Role creation and profile generation are done in the SAP S/4HANA development system and moved as a transport to the production system after testing. You assign these roles to users in the production system.

When maintaining security roles, authorizations, and profiles, you should follow these steps.

- You capture the Global Role transaction requirements during the analysis phase. The requirements outline the transactions and are categorized based on the business processes, subprocesses, and activity level, such as a display change.

- The Security Team maintains roles using the Profile Generator (transaction PFCG). In the PFCG, the roles are created to correspond to the process requirements. You add the tasks (reports and transactions) that belong to the related job function to the role menu.

- You define the activity level for each transaction on the Authorization tab for each role. Additionally, you add the organization level values as appropriate. The PFCG automatically builds the authorization profile that applies to the role.

- The roles are checked for segregation of duties (SoD) conflicts, tested, and then transported throughout the landscape and to production.

- You update the user assignment and generate a profile in the user master records.

SAP Role Types

SAP security roles are a collection of related activities and permissions stored together. From a usage perspective, you categorize such roles into several role types.

Master Role

A master role is a template containing the most granular collection of security restrictions (transaction code) that will eventually make up an end user's access in the SAP system. The master role does not define where (e.g., locations or data sets) you perform such transactions, so you do not assign them to the users directly.

Derived Roles

Derived roles are copied from the master roles to provide further restrictions on "where" you can perform a transaction (i.e., company code, plant). Derived role transactions and authorizations are inherited from the master role, but include additional restrictions identified in various organizational level fields. The transaction codes inherited from the master role restrict what a user can access.

A derived role is dependent on the master role. All transactional and nonorganizational field authorization values inherit from the master. You should maintain multiple roles (based on the master) with unique organizational field-level authorization values at the derived role level.

Single Role

Single roles contain common transactions used widely within the SAP environment that are not specific to a business process. Single roles can also be roles that have restricted transaction codes that only selected users will have access to, mainly for support if needed. Examples of these roles will be for security and BASIS support and emergency access roles.

Composite and Business Roles

These are a collection of derived and single roles making up a "basket" of functionality assigned to an end user. In the context of SAP security, the term *business role* is commonly used to associate a collection of single roles making up a position that could be assigned to end users. It is relevant for defining security roles applicable across multiple SAP systems. For example, a procurement-related role could include access to SAP S/4HANA, SRM, and portal.

There are two ways in which you can design the role types introduced here.

- Create a task-based role design where the small, modular role is applicable for a group of tasks the user is expected to perform; for example, purchase order processing, or material master maintenance.

- Create a job-based role design where roles are designed around jobs. Each job equates to one role, and that role provides all the access a user assigned to that job will need. For example, the purchase planner job role will include all the roles for purchase order processing as well as planning.

Table 7-3 gives a quick comparison of both role design approaches.

Table 7-3. *Two Approaches to Role Design*

Task-Based Role Design	Job-Based Role Design
Security is built based on small functionally definable tasks executed by a user (i.e., process cash receipts).	Security is built based on the job a user does (i.e., purchase planner).
A user might have more roles assigned, but there is a reduced risk of duplicate access.	A user gets a smaller number of roles; this increases the risk of granting functionality more than once.
Transaction codes required to complete the task are included in the same role.	Transaction codes and authorizations are duplicated in many roles.
User assignment is flexible; it is easy to grant additional access to only the tasks necessary.	Users might be granted more access than necessary because of "additional job" or backup responsibilities, thus there is less flexibility in role assignment.
Role maintenance is easier.	Role maintenance is often time-consuming.

Apart from the role design considerations already stated, there might also be a few additional restrictions that you want to enforce during security design:

- Nonorganizational levels like document types and field values.

- Organizational levels like specific sales or procurement organizations or plants.

Security for Nonproduction S/4HANA Systems

Nonproduction SAP S/4HANA systems often follow a simple role model that organizes access for the project teams. It is designed to be flexible yet maintains separation of the key functions. For example, roles for development access will be different from configuration access.

Table 7-4 lists some sample roles you will need to create in nonproduction SAP S/4HANA systems.

Table 7-4. *Sample Roles for Nonproduction S/4HANA Systems*

Role	Purpose
Configuration role	Full access to all the functional modules and configuration screens; they have fully functional access except for security, system administration, and ABAP development
BASIS role	Authorization to perform all system administration and standard BASIS functions
Security role	Authorization to create roles, generate profiles, perform role assignment, and perform user maintenance in the development environment
Development role	Authorization to perform all ABAP development and conversion activities as needed
Functional (Application) role	Authorization to use SAP user functions to simulate business scenarios for prototype and creating training materials; does not involve any authorization for configuration or security or BASIS-related tasks
Configuration + Functional + Developer role	Full access to functional modules, configuration screens, transactional data, and ABAP development
Training role	Authorization to full functional access related to end-user training

Additional References

- `https://help.sap.com/doc/6b11678926d3409bbfea88` `97cb34d10f/1809.002/en-US/INST_OP1809_FPS02.pdf`

- `https://help.sap.com/maintenanceplanner`

- `https://support.sap.com/sltoolset`

- `https://help.sap.com/doc/2b87656c4eee4284a5eb89` `76c0fe88fc/1809.002/en-US/CONV_OP1809_FPS02.pdf`

- `https://help.sap.com/doc/d7c2c95f2ed2402c9efa2f5` `8f7c233ec/1809.002/en-US/SEC_OP1809_FPS02.pdf`

- `https://help.sap.com/doc/6c3b63ec437f421cbfd92d` `10131cd685/1809.002/en-US/OPS_OP1809_FPS02.pdf`

CHAPTER 8

Organizational Change Management in S/4HANA

SAP S/4HANA implementation is often the biggest project an organization will undertake. It changes the way the organization works with internal as well as external stakeholders. Such changes will lead to the desired level of adoption if and only if they are fully understood and well-articulated during SAP S/4HANA implementation.

Managing this change effectively is the core objective OCM. Although there might be a tendency to downplay it, OCM) should be a key consideration from planning through the deployment phase of SAP S/4HANA.

If you look at the user engagement cycle shown in Figure 8-1, user engagement dips during the design/build/test cycles of SAP S/4HANA implementation. Initial excitement around SAP S/4HANA starts to dip as project teams work with occasional engagement with business users. During the deployment phase, reality sets in. As the system goes live, users start adjusting to the new way of working and find themselves in the aptly named valley of despair. This period of transition goes on for a few months. The system stabilizes soon after, as critical production issues are resolved up front. The support phase kicks in as users get used to the new way of working.

© Sanket Kulkarni 2019
S. Kulkarni, *Implementing SAP S/4HANA*, https://doi.org/10.1007/978-1-4842-4520-0_8

Having OCM covered up front keeps users engaged throughout the project life cycle. It helps set the right expectations and guides them during moments of despair during the deployment phases. It enables a smooth transition of users to the new SAP S/4HANA system and expedites user adoption.

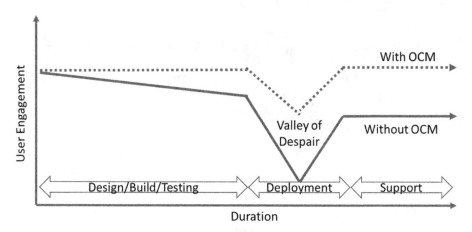

Figure 8-1. *User engagement cycle*

OCM Strategy

The key objective of an OCM exercise is to lead users to full adoption of the new solution and by doing so, lead the business to value realization by doing the following:

- Enabling all users affected by SAP S/4HANA to engage with the new platform.

- Communicating to all affected end users in advance using existing communication channels.

From an SAP S/4HANA implementation perspective, an OCM strategy should cover several important points.

- It should have a strong OCM governance and engagement model.

- It should have a proper communications and engagement strategy. This covers how you will communicate and engage with stakeholders throughout the project in terms of key decisions, issues, and benefits related to the SAP S/4HANA project.

- It should establish required support from stakeholders and change advocates. It ties into the preceding points, where key stakeholders should have a stake in OCM governance.

- It should outline the impact on the business and help in facilitating required skills, process changes, and cultural change.

- It should help with business readiness in terms of organizational design, role changes, and capability assessments. For example, most of the organization will move toward a centralized supply planning model while embarking on the SAP S/4HANA journey. This means that old siloed planning teams often need to be dismantled and rebuilt with a centralized focus. This leads to new job design and associated training and capability requirements.

- It should enable the required skills by meeting training and coaching needs.

The OCM exercise often begins with assessing the impact on the end users across the locations where SAP S/4HANA is going live. OCM assessment is conducted during the planning phase of the project. It is mainly a threefold exercise designed to cover all relevant points related to OCM strategy as stated earlier:

- Change impact assessment.

- Stakeholder assessment.

- Communications assessment.

Change Impact Assessment

The change impact assessment is an evaluation of the impact of the SAP S/4HANA project not just on the stakeholders, but also on processes. It also reviews associated skills and knowledge required once S/4HANA goes live, along with the necessary tool set. Note that we are referring to stakeholders here as all parties affected by this change. That includes internal as well as external stakeholders (customers, third parties). It is important that such an exercise should not be limited to end users within your organization, but include all relevant parties. Often, customers and third parties interface with the organization's ERP system. Moving to SAP S/4HANA might result in changes to the interface. Such changes, if not properly assessed and communicated, might result in the loss of business.

The change impact assessment evaluates how each of the stakeholder groups will be affected by the SAP S/4HANA project. It defines the impacts on stakeholders and supports the analysis for change intervention activities such as communications and training.

Such an assessment is conducted by the change management team members aligned with each process area. These members investigate the system, process, and role-level impacts of the SAP S/4HANA changes. Such analysis can highlight any major transition issues across the organization.

Table 8-1 shows a sample change impact assessment for the Finance Process area of SAP S/4HANA. Please note that based on the version of SAP S/4HANA used, this information might need to be updated.

Table 8-1. *Sample Change Impact Assessment*

Category	Description of the Change
Intercompany	The technical change will be seamless to end users. Reports and the security model must be updated accordingly.
Business Partner	S/4HANA manages the master data for clients, vendors, and employees centrally as Business Partners. This will result in changes to multiple users who currently have responsibility for data management across separate client, vendor, and employee tables. Change might be required for the vendor creation and approval process.
Fixed Assets Accounting	A potential new solution to manage open items at Clearing G/L accounts level, so users can be able to analyze and manage capitalizations as of today.
Cash Management Reporting	Change in forecasting and reporting: Change in the liquidity forecast capability and how short-term forecasts are created and reported via Fiori. Change how reports are displayed and executed (layout): Using role-based Fiori real-time apps (reports: daily global cash report and cash forecasts per entity or country).
Bank Account Management	Changes to Master Data Process: Changes to maintain and display old bank accounts data in Fiori SAP Bank Account Management as it introduces one central access point for bank account management. Certain T-codes will be replaced by Fiori app: Ability to create, display, and edit house banks using the Bank Account app.
Bank Statement Processing	Change to how reports are displayed as the existing report might be replaced by the Fiori Bank Statement Monitor app.

Please note that SAP S/4HANA offers much tighter integration across function areas, so change impact assessment across process areas is crucial. Although there are a lot of changes, especially in the Finance area, changes can also be significant in other areas. The change impact assessment should be a comprehensive exercise to identify all degrees (simple-to-complex) of process changes and their impact on stakeholder groups.

Stakeholder Assessment

Stakeholder assessment starts with identifying the affected stakeholders' groups and understanding their expectations and concerns regarding the change from the SAP S/4HANA project. Change management team members embedded into the process team help identify various user groups. For each process change (as provided in Table 8-1), affected user groups are identified and ranked by level of impact. For user groups affected by multiple changes, a higher ranking is given.

Stakeholder assessment often results in the matrix shown in Table 8-2.

Table 8-2. *Stakeholder Assessment Matrix*

Process Change	Stakeholder Groups/ Degree of Impact			
	Accounting	**Treasury**	**Budgeting**	**Customer Service**
Intercompany	High	High	High	Medium
Business Partner	High	Low	Low	Medium
Fixed Assets Accounting	High	Low	High	Low
Cash Management Reporting	Low	High	Low	Low
Bank Account Management	Medium	Low	Low	Low
Bank Statement Processing	Medium	Low	Low	Low

By understanding the stakeholder impacts across the process teams, you can identify the affected stakeholder groups along with their locations and plan to deliver tailored communications and training. As seen in the preceding example, the account department or stakeholder group is highly affected by the changes brought about by SAP S/4HANA, so a communications and training plan should be specifically targeted to this group. Other groups might require specialized training only in the affected areas.

Communication and Training Plan

As discussed earlier, a comprehensive change impact and stakeholder assessment allows you to define target areas with issues during the transition to SAP S/4HANA. Such issues can be addressed by outlining an adequate communications and training plan.

- A strong communications plan drives stakeholders' commitment to change through messages, activities, and the effective use of communication channels such as road shows, conferences, town halls, and so on.

  - A proper communication plan always drives ownership of the change communications at the business unit level if you are undergoing large-scale SAP S/4HANA transformation across countries and business units.

  - Although OCM governance can be managed by a central project organization, the right information and tools should be made available at the business unit level, so that stakeholders can further cascade it throughout the business unit.

- Please note that the communication plan should
  not end with a hypercare period. Successful
  organizations keep the communication plan open
  even in the stabilization phase as stakeholders are
  continually engaged in the SAP S/4HANA journey.

- A strong training plan equips stakeholders with the
  necessary knowledge and skills to adopt new ways of
  working with SAP S/4HANA.

  - One of the important aspects during training and
    performance support design is assessing the Fiori
    impact.

  - Fiori apps are much more intuitive than SAP
    graphical user interface (GUI) screens as they are
    role-specific. They break down the complexity of
    SAP GUI screens and often combine features from
    multiple SAP GUI transactions in one app, thus
    further simplifying the interaction with the end
    user.

  - Please also note that not all training scenarios are
    supported by Fiori, so it takes a clear understanding
    of the scenarios supported by Fiori apps vis-
    à-vis those not supported by Fiori apps. Some
    organizations also use repositories like Learning
    Hub for SAP S/4HANA. There are learning maps
    available for a specific S/4HANA version. It
    provides prebuilt learning content and jump starts
    your OCM exercise.

Communications Plan

Communications planning is about the management of messaging delivered via various communication channels to ensure maximum impact. Maximum impact is often achieved via targeted messaging for specific shareholder groups on specific affected areas. For example, the treasury group might be more interested in the cash management functionality in SAP S/4HANA, so your communication and training plan should reflect appropriate consideration.

An effective communication plan helps address the range of questions faced by relevant stakeholders during various phases of the program. During the planning phase, stakeholders might just be interested to know –the following:

- What is the background context of S/4HANA?

- What is the project about and what are its objectives?

- What is the overall timeline for the implementation?

- What are the expected benefits?

During the design, build, and test phase, stakeholders might be interested in the following:

- Where does my role fit into S/4HANA's future processes?

- What are the new functionalities of S/4HANA?

- How is it better than the existing system or process?

- How will I be affected by the changes?

- Where can I get more information?

As you move closer to the deployment, questions might change to ones more like these:

- What will be done to support my transition into the new functionality and the changes that will take place?

- When and where do I go for training?

- What will be happening in the weeks leading up to the go-live?

- How do I help others to adopt new ways of working?

- What will be done to sustain the change?

The communications plan should help you address the preceding questions in a timely manner and make sure that there are no communications gaps or misleading expectations from the program.

Based on the target stakeholder group, you can selectively use communication channels and tools. For sponsors, you might decide to use status reporting and quarterly communication calls. For line managers and work stream leads, monthly update meetings and conference calls might be enough. For team members, weekly team status meetings and reporting will do. For all team members, various communication channels such as reports, e-mails, town halls, orientation sessions, and off-site activities can be explored.

Based on the specific needs of the stakeholder group and orientation (operational, tactical, or strategic), communication methods and tools can be adjusted. Following communication tools and work, arrangements could be used that allow tight collaboration regardless of the time zone.

- Audio and video conferencing.

- Workday arrangements.

- Application sharing and remote presentation services (WebEx, NetMeeting).

Training Plan

The SAP S/4HANA program needs to deliver timely and relevant training based on stakeholder requirements. The focus of the training plan is to provide a flexible learning approach and enable users to be trained effectively in a short span of time. It starts with training assessment in terms of business process impacts, developing an SAP S/4HANA training curriculum, and creating a training design (e.g., ranging from simple Microsoft PowerPoint based to jazzy Web-based simulations), adding localization flavors if any, in terms of language, local requirements like taxation, regulatory requirement, and so on. It also includes consideration around training delivery, in person or using remote and associated logistics.

A blended approach allows for an integrated approach for both instructors and learners that encourages self-sufficient learners by incorporating performance support tools into the formal training program. Self-sufficient learners are taught how to leverage tools that will support their role beyond the immediate training curriculum during the stabilization phase. Learners will be given sufficient opportunities to apply the lessons learned in a training format.

Training design can include a variety of training modes, including the following:

- Instructor-led training (ILT) modules typically cover overview and process training materials

  - It contains a Microsoft PowerPoint presentation deck with simple graphics often augmented with instructor notes.

  - It does not typically include any simulations or exercises.

  - Assessments include multiple-choice questions that test the learners on knowledge, recall, and basic application with simple scenarios.

- System simulations

  - This includes a step-by-step demonstration of system activities along with practice modules.

- Job aids

  - These are user instructions containing generic and user-specific data needed to complete the transactions.

  - These contain screenshots and data inputs needed by specific transactions.

In summary, respective stakeholder groups move through the different adoption phases as your SAP S/4HANA program moves ahead. As shown in Figure 8-2, this gradual movement from Awareness ➤ Understanding ➤ Commitment ➤ Ownership should be closely aligned with the project phases of your SAP S/4HANA program.

Ideally, all the stakeholder groups should be at the level of ownership as you move toward postdeployment phases.

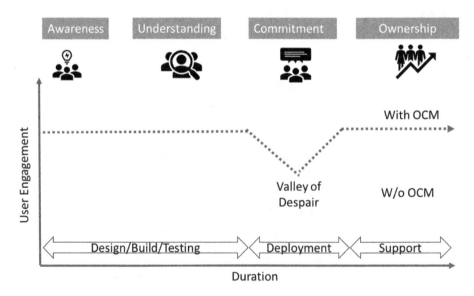

Figure 8-2. Adoption phases

Table 8-3 gives a summary view of OCM activities and associated adoption phases throughout the life cycle of an SAP S/4HANA project.

Table 8-3. *Summary of Organization Change Management Activities*

Adoption Phase	Project Phase	OCM Activities	Stakeholder Impact
Awareness	Analyze	Based on the requirement sessions, change impact assessment along with stakeholder assessment is conducted for the process areas. Target organization structure including jobs and teams is defined.	Resulting change strategy leads to the development of the communications and training plan customized for stakeholder groups.
Awareness	Design	Training curriculum (including courses, modules) is finalized. Key stakeholder contacts are identified.	Resultant training curriculum and design are sent for preview to key stakeholder contacts. Communication channels and tools are finalized. Communications with stakeholders are kicked off. Organization structure is finalized.

(continued)

Table 8-3. (*continued*)

Adoption Phase	Project Phase	OCM Activities	Stakeholder Impact
Understanding	Build	Training content is built and reviewed with SMEs. Preparation for training events (i.e., environment, logistics, schedule) is complete with trainers identified. Deployment of the changes in the organization structure and jobs is designed.	Collaboration with stakeholders to communicate to end users using existing channels is in place. Communications using various channels (roadshow, town halls, meetings, etc.) are kicked off.
Understanding	Test	Training schedule is finalized. Training content is further refined.	Communications continue. The training schedule is published to the stakeholders. Training is executed to superuser groups and feedback is sought. Proposed changes in the organization structure are communicated.

(*continued*)

Table 8-3. (*continued*)

Adoption Phase	Project Phase	OCM Activities	Stakeholder Impact
Commitment	Deploy	Performance support and user instruction materials are prepared and published.	Online and offline resources for deployment and support are published to the stakeholder groups. Go-live communications are sent out. Hypercare and stabilization activities are in place and well communicated. Changes in jobs and organization structure are in place.

CHAPTER 9

Fiori in S/4HANA

In early 2007, the first-generation iPhone was launched by Apple with much fanfare. Who would have thought that over the intervening years, the smartphone market would explode and we would be able to order groceries from the comfort of our homes? Whole marketplaces have moved to online and you can pretty much do business on the phone. As consumers moved toward slick UIs offered by a multitude of mobile apps at a much faster pace, enterprise applications such as monolith ERPs took much longer to adapt.

The UI revolution has affected significantly the way companies do business, manufacture and track goods, ship products, and reach out to customers. With mobility becoming the default option for many, customers and employees alike, the need to have a mobile-centric UI was obvious. Not just the back-end ERP has to be mobile-enabled; any other IT applications in the landscape are now expected to follow the same UI design principles.

It has led to business-centric mobile-enabled devices like smartphones, tablets, and even smartwatches, as well as applications (or apps). Such applications inherently work across multiple types of devices seamlessly and are expected to provide the same user experience whether someone is accessing the application on a smartphone or a tablet. Such applications are also designed for access from anywhere and on any mobile-enabled devices.

© Sanket Kulkarni 2019
S. Kulkarni, *Implementing SAP S/4HANA*, https://doi.org/10.1007/978-1-4842-4520-0_9

For example, perhaps your sales representative is having a meeting at a customer's location and needs real-time information on the next available delivery dates. In this case, he can always pull up his tablet and access a Fiori application on sales order delivery. He can quickly pull up all the details in front of the customer and can close the sale on the go.

The mobility trend has also been recognized by SAP and it led to complete revamp of the traditional SAP GUI. Old SAP front-end applications were designed with one transaction for multiple roles. It led to exposing all data and functions associated with that transaction to all the users with requisite access. On top of that, there were multiple entry points for the user, so there was an inconsistency in the UI across applications.

If you take a simple transaction such as Sales Order Creation (VA01) in the traditional SAP GUI, you can see so many fields to populate and so many screens to be navigated. The overall look was very clumsy and it often took a long time to create one sales order that was complete in all aspects.

Starting with Business Suite on HANA, new SAP UX technologies (SAP Fiori being just one of them) were introduced. As SAP S/4HANA matures, offerings under Fiori have been expanded with more than 7,000 ready-to-use apps along with easy customizations.

Key Changes

The following are some of the key changes SAP introduced with Fiori.

- *Role-based applications:* This means there are apps for each role, thus exposing only relevant data and functions for that specific role. For example, the role Internal Sales Representative - SAP_BR_INTERNAL_SALES_REP will give you access for tracking sales orders as well as other Fiori apps related to managing sales contracts and inquiries.

- *Single entry point for the user:* This means a consistent UX following common design principles across all devices: smartphones, tablets, and even smartwatches. Taking the same example as before, Internal Sales Representative will have access to the My Sales Overview app, a dashboard for all sales-related activities such as handling sales quotations, analyzing sales order fulfillment performance, and so on. She can also dive deep into the details of specific problem areas, by clicking on individual cards as shown in Figure 9-1.

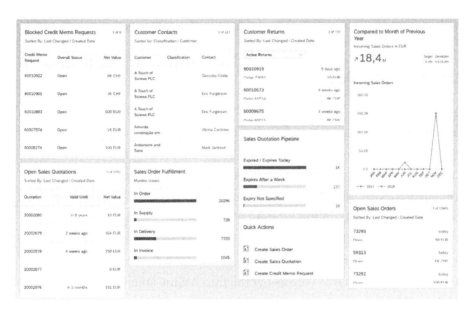

Figure 9-1. *My Sales Overview Fiori app*

Fiori App Categories

Fiori apps are divided into three categories.

Transactional Apps

Transactional apps give access to each user to run SAP transactions on desktops or laptops and mobile devices and tablets. These are the apps you use to create and update business documents or perform specific business tasks. These are role-based simplified views that mirror transactions in the old SAP ERP system. For example, the Purchaser transactional app covers transactions related to a purchase order, purchase requisition, and so on.

Analytical Apps

Analytical apps provide role-based insight into real-time operations of your business by aggregating key figures so that you can closely monitor your most important KPIs in real time and react immediately based on changes in market conditions or operations. SAP analytical apps provide predelivered KPIs and insight-to-action scenarios. You can also define your own KPIs based on the modeling framework.

For example, a strategic buyer can access analytical apps related to overdue purchase order items or off-contract spends. He can also monitor invoice price variance as well as overall purchasing spend.

Fact Sheets

Fact sheets display master data or business documents in display mode. Fact sheets are often called from other apps like analytical apps in Fiori launchpad. Also, you can search master data or business documents in the Fiori launchpad like Google Search. Fact sheets are called by selecting the search result. You can further drill down into its details. For example, a production planner can access production order, work center, and resource details from a single fact sheet. She can also search by a specific material and then further drill down to respective production orders and their associated documents like good movements.

Fiori Architecture

As seen in Figure 9-2, the Fiori architecture consists of the SAP Gateway communicating with the back-end S/4HANA system and SAP Web Dispatcher.

The SAP Web Dispatcher lies between the Internet and your SAP system. It is the entry point for HTTP(s) requests into your system, which consists of one or more SAP NetWeaver application servers. It also feeds data to front-end applications where it is Fiori apps modeled using SAP UI5 technology, SAP Screen Personas or any other UX technology. Users can further access these apps on any devices such as a desktop, tablet, or smartphone.

HANA DB enabled by CDS feeds into the SAP S/4HANA ABAP layer. CDS provides programming features such as data definitions, query language, and data manipulation logic often programmed using Structured Query Language (SQL) statements in SAP HANA.

The SAP S/4HANA ABAP layer consists of the business logic the and associated back-end data. It is also responsible for security aspects such as users, roles, and authorizations.

InA Search offers search engine functionality (like Google Search) whenever you deal with large amounts of data; for example, material descriptions, service incidents, and so on. Fact sheets use this functionality, which makes direct calls to the SAP S/4HANA ABAP layer for faster retrieval times.

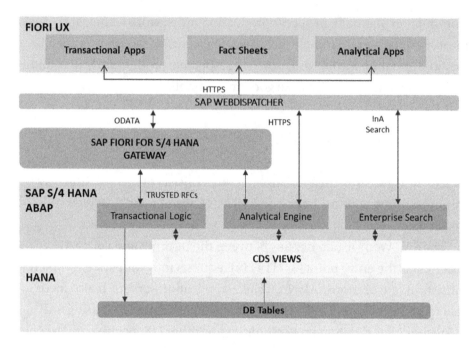

Figure 9-2. *Fiori architecture*

There are two types of deployment options for SAP Fiori.

- *Embedded deployment option:* In this option, you
  deploy Fiori architecture components like SAP Gateway
  server, SAP UI5, and a Fiori UI add-on in the same
  environment as in SAP S/4HANA.

  - This option means reduced costs due to a single
    landscape, although it becomes overly dependent
    (in terms of versions and scalability) on the back-
    end SAP S/4HANA server configuration.

- *Hub deployment (recommended option):* In this option,
  you deploy Fiori architecture components like SAP
  Gateway server, SAP UI5, and a Fiori UI add-on in a
  different environment than SAP S/4HANA.

- Often termed noninvasive installation, this option does not require any downtime on the back-end SAP S/4HANA system.

- With clear separation on UI and business systems, it is a much simpler architecture, although it requires higher maintenance.

- Note that there is no direct access to the back-end system in this option but only via the SAP Gateway hub.

Implementing SAP Fiori

You should start by defining the SAP UX strategy for your organization. The SAP UX strategy takes a broader view in terms of all available SAP UX technologies and how they fit into your organization's UX vision. UX visioning exercises often try to address these questions from your organization's perspective:

- What are your employees' UX expectations?

- What are external users' and customers' UX expectations?

- What are the UX opportunities available in specific business domains? For example, you want to enable your customers for order tracking via the dedicated customer portal.

- What are the source systems that will pass data to those UX opportunities?

- What are the key security considerations?

- What are the key performance considerations?

- Are there any device-based limitations (e.g., company-owned devices or any smartphones)?

Potential UX opportunities are further prioritized with business and IT stakeholders. Such a conversation is often enabled with rapid prototyping. You can also use the SAP Fiori discovery tool to assess application usage in your environments and generate recommendations for Fiori apps.

As your UX vision begins to develop, you will be able to shortlist critical UX opportunities. These opportunities fall into one of the three categories of scenarios.

- Consumer-grade UX for new applications. An example would be a new customer portal to enable online ordering that would require UI design from scratch.

- Renewal of existing applications by applying SAP UX for common business scenarios. Transactional apps often fit into this category.

- Enabling users with critical business scenarios by providing operational insights faster. Analytical apps and to some extent fact sheets fit into this category.

There are several SAP UX technologies on offer, Fiori being the predominant one.

- *SAP WebDynpro/SAP NetWeaver Business Client:* You might recall this from your old SAP ERP systems. It is still available, but not mobility-enabled.

- *SAP Fiori:* Standard FIORI apps (transactional, analytical, and fact sheets) are offered by SAP with limited customization. It closely integrates with the SAP S/4HANA back-end system and offers portability across all devices.

- *SAP UI5:* This is used to renew existing transactions and generate new business scenarios. It is developed on HTML5 and can be integrated into multiple back ends. Although portability is offered across all devices, you will need extensive design effort to map user requirements to screens before you write even a single line of code.

- *SAP Screen Personas:* This is used for a limited set of users with very specific business requirements. Being highly configurable, it allows users the capability to configure their own personas for specific transactions.

- *SAP Mobility Platforms:* This is used for complex mobility scenarios like developing customer portals from scratch. It also covers standard and custom transactions and requires specific design cycles to develop screens. It can integrate with multiple devices and offers extensive customization.

To make a decision on the appropriate SAP UX technology that serves your purpose, start by asking these questions.

- Does your business requirement need access to mobile devices to function efficiently?

- How granular is your requirement?

  - For the same transaction, if personas (i.e., user profiles) have different information needs, then you should create multiple apps so that each user gets a tailored experience. It is called the decomposition process because it breaks down complex megatransactions into simplified apps.

- On the other hand, you could combine multiple transactions and present them in a single app to support the user to achieve an outcome only possible by combining two experiences otherwise found in separate transactions. This is called the composition process, the process of combining multiple similar and related transactions into one single integrated app.

- Will it be used on low-connectivity areas, in an online as well as an offline mode? Only specific Fiori apps provide an offline mode, so it becomes a deciding factor.

- Is it a business-to-business (B2B), business-to-consumer (B2C), or business-to-employee (B2E) scenario? Here are some typical examples:

  - B2B: Customer or supplier portals.

  - B2C: Order management, EMI/loan tracking, and complaint management.

  - B2E: Employee self-service, performance management, and learning management.

- Which devices it is supposed to work on?

  - Options include bring-your-own-device (BYOD), choose-your-own-device (CYOD), and company-issued, personal enabled (COPE) devices.

  - Note that data confidentiality considerations become more complex in SAP Fiori applications extended to mobile devices or devices that are not owned by the organization.

- How should security of data on devices and in transit be managed?

You should then ask whether there are existing Fiori apps for the same use case. If not, you can develop a custom app using the SAP UI5 framework. If it's really going to be accessed only on the desktops, then you can even develop one using SAP WebDynpro.

Please note that not all SAP S/4HANA transaction codes or functionalities have corresponding Fiori apps, so it makes sense to assess up front to what extent your UI needs are satisfied via Fiori apps.

Here are a few other key considerations.

- The infrastructure must be scaled to support Fiori (OData service call) to prevent performance issues. That warrants performance testing of Fiori apps during test cycles.

- Compatibility issues with other web browsers should also be thoroughly tested (Chrome works better with Fiori).

If you are going to develop custom Fiori apps using the SAP UI5 framework, you should be aware of Fiori design principles.

Here are key Fiori design principles outlined by SAP.

- It should be role-based.

  - Designs for what I do.

  - Understands tasks I need to do and helps me do them better.

  - Builds from insights within my business networks.

- It should be responsive.

  - Works seamlessly across all screen sizes and devices that have an HTML5-compatible browser.

  - Adjusts their layout based on the available screen real estate.

- Supports multiple interaction modes, such as keyboards, mouse, and touch-based inputs.

- Works independently of platform or ecosystem (Windows, Android, or iOS).

- It should be simple.

  - Helps the user complete tasks quickly and easily.

  - Emphasizes a 1:1:3 approach: one user, one use case, and three screens (desktop, tablet, and mobile).

- It should be coherent.

  - Have the same design footprint and thus the same look and feel.

  - Speaks the same design language.

- It should provide instant value.

  - Follows the same design pattern across apps.

  - Makes it easier for users to adopt the new UI quickly.

Fiori Configuration

Once you short-list the Fiori apps for enablement, you can follow these steps for Fiori configuration.

1. Verify and prepare the SAP back end.

   a. It involves validating prerequisites and deploying necessary SAP notes.

2. Infrastructure installation.

    a. Depending on your chosen deployment scenario—
        embedded or hub-based—various architectural
        components such as SAP NetWeaver Gateway, or
        SAP UI5 add-on are to be installed.

    b. After installation of the SAP Gateway server,
        necessary connections are made to the SAP
        S/4HANA back-end system.

3. Network and security configuration.

    a. Because SAP Fiori apps enable users to access SAP
        back-end data from a variety of devices located
        in different networks, the connectivity channels
        between the SAP Fiori apps and SAP Business Suite
        must be secured.

    b. This involves enabling external and mobile access
        and configuring user roles and authorizations.

4. Standard application and workflow installation and
    configuration.

    a. Involves enablement of standard Fiori apps

5. Launch page customizing and branding using the
    Theme Designer. For example, you can put your
    logo on the customer-facing apps.

Fiori Authorizations

The authorization concept of SAP Fiori is related to the authorizations
needed to access the S/4HANA ABAP back-end server as well as OData
services in the SAP Gateway server.

While launching a SAP Fiori app, the request is sent from SAP Fiori Launchpad to the SAP Gateway server via Web Dispatcher. Once the initial authentication is complete, a security session is established between the SAP Fiori Launchpad and the SAP Gateway server. This allows SAP Fiori apps to send OData service requests to the SAP S/4HANA ABAP back-end server. These requests are communicated securely by using trusted RFC (Remote Function Call). You will therefore need authorizations to start SAP Fiori apps as well as to use the business logic and data from the SAP S/4HANA back-end system.

Additional References

- https://help.sap.com/doc/61634ead9e5144b89e7eca2b1d4b8bce/1809.002/en-US/UITECH_OP1809_FPS02.pdf

- https://fioriappslibrary.hana.ondemand.com/sap/fix/externalViewer/

- https://experience.sap.com/documents/sap-fiori-ux-architecture-for-s4h.pdf

- https://blogs.sap.com/2016/09/21/fiori-front-end-server-20-important-links/

- https://experience.sap.com/fiori-design/

- https://saplumira.com/

CHAPTER 10

Embedded Analytics in S/4HANA

One of the key benefits you can reap from SAP S/4HANA implementation is better operational reporting and financial closing processes. Deriving insights from a volume of data is often a nightmare for frontline managers as well as executives. The Embedded Analytics feature of SAP S/4HANA is one of the critical value drivers for moving to SAP S/4HANA.

Historically, SAP ERP systems lacked capabilities to generate analytics directly on the back-end system in real time. Due to lack of such capability (often constrained by technological limitations of the relational database management system [RDBMS]), organizations often resorted to setting up EDW using SAP Business Warehouse (BW). It was not an easy solution to build and maintain. It required tremendous effort to sync operational data at the regular intervals and often resulted in duplication of the data across the organization. Maintenance was costly and fraught with risks of data errors (remember issues with queues and data transfer). Even with such hassle, the organization could not get what it wanted—real-time operational insights to help with business execution. SAP BW reports were based on the historical data and often provided time-lagged information.

That's why the Embedded Analytics feature is so exciting; it provides faster organizational insights directly from the HANA database without any need for duplication. In a new SAP S/4HANA world, the role of SAP BW

© Sanket Kulkarni 2019
S. Kulkarni, *Implementing SAP S/4HANA*, https://doi.org/10.1007/978-1-4842-4520-0_10

(now being called BW4/HANA) has moved to provide more strategic and tactical reporting and real-time operational analytics has now become the domain of Embedded Analytics.

Now, let us look at how technology has influenced operational reporting capabilities in SAP. In the past, operational managers relied on options like Standard Reports, Logistics Information Systems–based reports, Report Builder, SAP Query, and custom ABAP Reports. As SAP moved to Suite on HANA, the HANA Live views provided much more flexible options to build operational reports, leveraging the power of HANA, and thus providing much better analytical reports and visibility into the KPIs.

You can consider Embedded Analytics the SAP S/4HANA version of virtual data models (VDMs), which are built using CDS. Like HANA Live views from Suite on HANA, the CDS views can also be accessed via the SAP BI tools apart from the Embedded Analytics feature in SAP S/4HANA.

Understanding CDS Views

CDS is the set of services used to define and consume operational data. With Embedded Analytics, SAP now provides packaged CDS views for transactional and master data that can be used as the foundation to access data from underlying physical tables. Such prepackaged CDS views can be extended as needed. Although reporting needs vary for each organization, highly customizable CDS views with preconfigured content can help in jump-starting SAP analytics implementations.

Embedded Analytics implementations start with defining the operational reports that the organization is currently using or planning to use in the future. Operational reporting is about providing the necessary information for business users. It helps them to perform their day-to-day operations efficiently. Thus, it requires real-time data with access to many transactional tables.

Some of the common examples of operational reporting are open orders, daily sales outstanding (DSO), inventory levels, material usage analysis, and so on. Such data help address specific questions such as these:

- What orders do I need to ship today?

- Can I see the orders that have been shipped but not yet billed?

That's where operational reporting covered by Embedded Analytics differs from Business Intelligence, which is covered by BW4/HANA. Business Intelligence helps to answer questions such as these:

- How can I ship my products more efficiently?

- How am I doing on crucial operational metrics, say service levels or inventory turns over the medium to long term?

Embedded Analytics is about discovering process inefficiencies in real time and acting on them instantly. As compared to the time-lagged insights derived from Business Intelligence, Embedded Analytics is about generating insights in real time, thus improving the effectiveness of the user actions.

This does not mean that operational reporting is the exclusive domain of Embedded Analytics. Insights generated by SAP Embedded Analytics can be consumed through various reporting tools in the SAP domain such as SAP Advanced Analysis for Office, SAP Lumira, SAP Predictive Analysis, SAP Fiori, SAP Smart Business Cockpits, SAP Design Studio, SAP Cloud for Analytics, KPI Modeling Apps (Fiori), Query Browser/Query Builder and even EPM for planning and consolidation.

Now, let us understand the key features offered by SAP Embedded Analytics. Here are a set of analytics features that are well embedded in SAP S/4HANA.

- *SAP Smart Business Cockpits (SBC):* This is an operational dashboard built using SAP Fiori design principles. It contains a set of KPIs, helps prioritize actions for the user, and provides insights on the go. For example, you could have a dashboard with a set of KPIs, analyze the ones that need attention, and act in the same dashboard for a user.

- *Query Browser:* Query Browser is a Fiori app that allows you to search and execute specific analytical queries.

- *Query Designer:* The Query Designer, not to be confused with BEx Query Designer, is a Fiori app that allows you to create and manage analytics queries.

- *Analytics Fiori apps:* Prebuilt Analytics Fiori apps (mostly standard) are used for operational analysis.

Data generated in Embedded Analytics can be presented in a variety of ways to the user. Some of the options available in Fiori Launchpad are given in Figure 10-1.

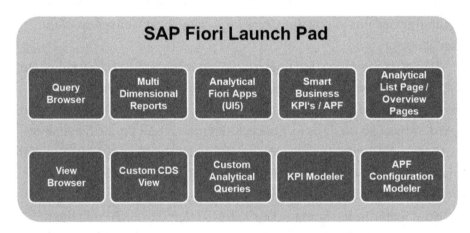

Figure 10-1. *Reporting options in the Fiori Launchpad*

- Multidimensional reports allow users to slice and dice, sort, and filter functionalities. You can also build personalized views and set up navigation to other Fiori apps as needed.

- SAP Smart Business KPIs are the KPI tiles on the Fiori Launchpad providing quantitative information with various drill-downs by selected dimensions.

- Analytical List Page offers filters to prioritize on the most critical areas with operational details.

- Overview Pages are often used to present the essential information at a glance (instead of opening many different transactions), thus offering a combination of analytical and transactional data.

- Analytical SAP Fiori apps are the Fiori apps predefined by SAP, using Fiori floorplans and UI5 controls implemented for specific analytical use cases.

- Query Browser lists the analytical queries assigned to the current user with In-App Search.

There are also other options to present data generated by Embedded Analytics tools. SAP BusinessObjects offers BI Launch Pad with functionalities including the following

- *Crystal Reports:* This provides a custom reporting environment with the ability to access data from various sources with design and formatting features.

- *WEBI (Web Intelligence):* This is often used for ad-hoc reporting.

- *Analytics for Office:* This Microsoft Excel add-in has the ability to connect to SAP S/4HANA.

Other visualization and planning tools such as SAP Lumira, Tableau, and SAP BPC also leverage reports generated by Embedded Analytics.

If you want to visualize an Embedded Analytics architecture, it has two broad-based components. The back-end layer consists of HANA DB accessed by VDMs and CDS views. The front-end layer consists of a range of options including Fiori Launchpad, SAP Business Objects, or visualization tools offered by SAP.

CDS Implementation

While implementing the Embedded Analytics functionality, you should start by understanding CDS features as well as available standard CDS content. CDS holds programming features such as data definitions, query language, and data manipulation logic often programmed using SQL statements in SAP HANA. That's why CDS is often called the brain of the Embedded Analytics functionality. Because CDS allows the ability to create views as per the organization's reporting requirements, the majority of the customizations happen in this area during the implementation.

You can broadly classify CDS views into three categories.

- *Basic views:* Used to interact with the HANA database for fetching data.

- *Composite views:* Typically created on top of basic views using joins, associations, and calculations, often to represent operational reporting across multiple functional areas.

- *Consumption views:* Created on top of composite views and expose data to various analytical tools (Lumira, Analysis for Excel, Fiori, etc.). These are the views that your business users will see and consume.

Here are the steps for implementing SAP Embedded Analytics functionality.

1. Start by identifying your reporting requirements, especially operational reporting requirements. Remember that the Business Intelligence system, an EDW, will continue to meet your tactical and strategic needs.

2. Once you identify any reporting requirements, check whether there is already any standard Fiori analytical app that fits the requirement.

3. If not, check whether any existing Fiori analytical app can be extended easily.

4. If an app needs further customization and extension, identify a data source or search an appropriate CDS view. Once customized, review whether you can meet the same needs by creating an analytical query via Query Designer based on the custom CDS view. You can also publish a custom CDS view to the Business Objects or OData service (to be used by any mobile application).

5. Conduct performance tuning of custom CDS views by exposing only required fields, performing expensive operations (e.g., calculated fields) only after data reduction (filtering, aggregation), avoiding joins and filters on calculated fields, and limiting the amount of data persisted in Embedded Analytics as compared to the overall data volume of the system.

6. If your reporting requirements are very complex, you should consider developing an SAP ABAP report or custom Fiori Analytical app.

Integration with SAP Analytics

SAP Analytics strategy is based on the Native HANA based on CDS views developed using an SQL approach. It means that your custom CDS views can be reused across various analytical offerings in SAP space, be it SAP BusinessObjects Analytics suite, SAP Lumira Design Studio, SAP Analytics Cloud, or SAP BW/4HANA. Benefits are faster deployments, reduced memory footprint, and overall reduction in the total cost of ownership. Let us discuss how SAP S/4HANA Embedded Analytics integrates with various components of SAP Analytics offerings.

SAP BusinessObjects Analytics Suite and SAP Lumira Design Studio

The SAP BusinessObjects Analytics suite provides analytics for SAP BW/4HANA and integrates with SAP S/4HANA Embedded Analytics using a standard interface.

SAP Analytics Cloud

There exists a standard interface between SAP S/4HANA Embedded Analytics and SAP Analytics Cloud. Some advantages of using SAP Analytics Cloud are as follows:

- Data stays in the source system. Only metadata is stored in the SAP Analytics Cloud. There are no data transfers needed from source to the browser.

- Data can be queried directly from the browser, so sensitive data stays entirely within the organization.

CDS Analytical Query views created using Embedded Analytics are accessed via SAP Analytics Cloud Stories. For example, assume that you have created a custom CDS view for monitoring the delivery performance of your sales orders. The logic for calculating delivery performance is embedded into the SQL programs associated with the CDS view.

Now, you can associate the same CDS view with an SAP Analytics Cloud model configured explicitly for monitoring SAP Delivery Performance. The same SAP Analytics Cloud model is further associated with the Delivery Performance cloud story accessed by business users. That way, your business users can access the same operational reporting via SAP Analytics Cloud as in the Embedded Analytics front end (e.g., Fiori Launchpad) using the same CDS view.

SAP BW/4HANA

Whereas the SAP S/4HANA Embedded Analytics feature is for real-time operational reporting embedded in the transaction system itself, SAP BW/4 HANA is an EDW solution that often caters to cross-system, cross-functional reporting requirements.

SAP does not recommend using Embedded Analytics for EDW use cases. You should not consider Embedded Analytics as a replacement for SAP BW/4HANA. Instead, it should be viewed as an augmentation of existing analytical capability with instant insights.

There are three ways in which SAP BW/4HANA can extract data from the SAP S/4HANA system:

- Classic extraction using data sources.

- ABAP CDS extraction (where Embedded Analytics CDS views can be reused).

- DB table replication using the SLT layer.

Once data is extracted from SAP source systems (e.g., S/4HANA, SRM, etc.) by using one of these options, it is imported into InfoCubes within the SAP Business Intelligence system. BEx queries are created using these InfoCubes. BEx queries offer a many customizations to users so that specific views are created based on extracted data according to business requirements. Graphical reports can also be built based on the BEx queries using the SAP BusinessObjects front-end interface.

From an architectural standpoint, there are two scenarios in which BW/4HANA integrates with SAP S/4HANA.

Scenario 1: SAP S/4HANA Embedded Analytics and SAP BW4/HANA in Two Different Instances

In this case, SAP BW4/HANA consumes Embedded Analytics CDS views having real-time access to the transaction and master data residing in the S/4HANA system. It can further enrich data from Embedded Analytics CDS views with managed master data (e.g., hierarchies). Transactional data from Embedded Analytics can also be enhanced with data stored in the Datastore object. For example, historical sales order data can be appended to real-time sales order performance data to indicate trends in sales.

Scenario 2: SAP BW Embedded in SAP S/4HANA

In this case, you can use SAP S/4HANA Embedded Analytics CDS views without any further investments, thus leveraging BEx capabilities. All SAP S/4HANA CDS views are automatically exposed and can be used in the BEx Query Designer to define custom queries. It's a quick way to add BW functionality without using BW modeling objects.

Additional References

- https://rapid.sap.com/bp/BP_S4H_ANA
- https://help.sap.com/viewer/cc0c305d2fab47bd808
  adcad3ca7ee9d/7.5.6/en-US/630ce9b386b84e80bfade
  96779fbaeec.html
- https://blogs.sap.com/2016/03/10/sap-s4hana-
  embedded-analytics-a-detailed-walkthrough-
  part-13/
- https://scn.sap.com/community/s4hana/blog/
  2015/11/23/unified-solution-sap-s4hana-
  embedded-analytics-sap-business-warehouse-
  powered-by-sap-hana
- https://scn.sap.com/community/s4hana/blog/
  2016/04/07/the-end-of-sap-business-warehouse-
  in-the-context-of-sap-s4hana-is-not-in-sight

CHAPTER 11

Deployment and Governance Strategy for S/4HANA

SAP S/4HANA implementation is one of the most significant business transformations you will ever undertake. So far, we have been discussing the "what" of SAP S/4HANA in terms of process and technology components. Process components include functional items, development changes, and related data considerations. Technology components include technical architecture considerations, including Fiori and Embedded Analytics.

With a governance and deployment strategy, we discuss the "how" of SAP S/4HANA implementation. We address a way to deploy SAP S/4HANA along with the aspects of governance and organization structure needed to support such deployment.

Assessing process and technology components is important, but setting up an overall governance and deployment strategy up front is equally essential. You should start discussions on the deployment strategy as early as the planning or assessment phase. Such analyses are held in the form of workshops with principal business and IT stakeholders. Inputs from process and technology components are taken into consideration.

For example, if you are a pharmaceutical company starting to use SAP S/4HANA, longer test cycles are a norm due to additional validation

© Sanket Kulkarni 2019
S. Kulkarni, *Implementing SAP S/4HANA*, https://doi.org/10.1007/978-1-4842-4520-0_11

requirements. Such consideration affects your deployment strategy in terms of how the test phase is planned in light of the overall program.

The biggest driver affecting deployment strategy is the implementation approach. Depending on the approach for SAP S/4HANA—Greenfield, Brownfield, or consolidation—activities planned during each deployment phase change.

Three-Pronged Approach

We consider the three-pronged approach while developing a deployment strategy for SAP S/4HANA. The optimal deployment solution hinges on business, scope (process and technology), and budget for the SAP S/4HANA implementation program.

- Business

  - The schedule is derived to ensure business continuity. It should cause minimal impact to the operations and minimal business disruption, and thus little impact to customers.

  - Business culture drives how organizations respond to change. You should assess whether you are open to the sudden change like a big-bang go-live or slow and steady transformation with long-term rollouts.

  - You should also consider decision-making style: whether you have headquarters driving template decisions or consensus-driven decision making, which takes longer but has greater likelihood of buy-in from the stakeholders. Consensus style is going to take a long time to secure signoffs, which should be considered during deployment.

- Accordingly, organization structure changes are minimized. No legal entity or business unit is split unless needed. Communications are planned early for affected customers and third parties.

- You should also consider external factors such as how your competitors are adopting SAP S/4HANA transformations. If market forces are demanding a comprehensive online strategy, then you might need to expedite deployments. If you are in the middle of a merger and acquisition spree, it also affects your deployment strategy.

- Scope (process and technology)

  - It is ensured that SAP S/4HANA covers the entire process and technology scope.

  - The process is simplified and focused on the back-to-standard or best practices.

  - The scope is prioritized and strictly monitored via change control mechanism. It is closely aligned with the business case.

- Budget and cost

  - Deployment speed is derived based on meaningful parameters such as users or business revenue. Pilot deployments are done to accelerate learnings, at the same time accounting for localizations.

  - The longer it takes to implement SAP S/4HANA throughout the organization, the more expensive it becomes. It also delays the benefits you are expecting to derive from the implementation. Thus, it weakens the overall SAP S/4HANA business case.

- Some organizations opt for overlaps or parallel deployments to reduce the overall deployment timeline, and thus reduce costs.

Deployment Constraints

Once you complete the deployment assessment based on the three factors listed earlier, you should be able to identify deployment constraints at first. They are further categorized into hard and soft constraints.

- Hard constraints

  - These are the constraints that cannot be compromised.

  - For example, the SAP S/4HANA implementation journey should not be more than three years, or you need to front-load some specific functionality to justify the value proposition for SAP S/4HANA.

- Soft constraints

  - These are the guardrails that are used to provide guidance, although they are open for interpretation or adjustments.

  - For example, pilot deployment should achieve 80% of targeted functionality, or we should follow best practices whenever possible, or customization should be backed by legal or regulatory considerations only.

Deployment Scenarios

There are multiple deployment scenarios when it comes to implementing SAP S/4HANA. We discuss them one-by-one in terms of the pros and cons of each.

Value and Functionality-Based Deployment

In this model, you focus on faster value realization, thus minimizing risk, so you introduce functionalities in the SAP S/4HANA production system in a phased manner. For example, financial consolidation is one of the critical priorities for a business you recently acquired. You would like to integrate financials first, moving on to supply chain functionalities later. Such consideration might drive you to go with Central Finance first, then start the rest of the SAP S/4HANA functionalities later.

Such a staggered approach of introducing the functionality often helps to isolate user impacts to specific modules, thus minimizing impact to external customers or third parties. The issue with this approach is that it requires very complex interim processes. Throw-away integrations between legacy and SAP S/4HANA have to build to support end-to-end business processes.

Big-Bang Deployment

A big-bang deployment is an all-in approach with all end-to-end business processes deployed in a single phase. All customers, as well as business units, move to SAP S/4HANA at once. For small and medium-sized enterprises, it is an attractive consideration, provided limited organization resources are spent with a clear line of sight. For large organizations starting a comprehensive digital transformation (e.g., SAP S/4HANA led the project with other components like SFDC, Hybris, or Ariba), it comes with a lot of risks in terms of cutover strategy, data transformation, and change management.

Benefits of this approach are apparent lower cost due to the truncated implementation schedule. This means that business case is straightforward and can be achieved faster as key functionalities start delivering value from Day 1.

The issue with this approach is that it leads to significant operational disruption unless managed properly and it affects all users and customers at once. The SAP S/4HANA solution is stabilized postimplementation and often has a volatile transition period until the organization completely aligns with SAP S/4HANA.

Geography-Driven Deployment

Geography-driven deployment involves deploying complete end-to-end processes in SAP S/4HANA only for a specific geography. Once stabilized and learning is captured, it is further deployed to the other geographies. The benefits of this approach are that you can capture learning and stabilize the SAP S/4HANA solution in the pilot site before rolling it out to the rest of the geographical units. However, global templates (or complete end-to-end processes) have to be built up front along with throw-away interim procedures. Such an arrangement also affects your legacy systems, as they also have to selectively process data in geographical units that are yet not on the SAP S/4HANA system. A long, drawn-out geography-driven rollout model can be taxing to organizational resources and can further delay the benefits outlined in the business case.

Business Unit-Driven Deployment

Business-driven deployment focuses on deploying SAP S/4HANA in the specific business unit at the time regardless of any geographical considerations. You will still implement all end-to-end business processes as required by a particular business unit. Such a focused rollout model minimizes customer impact, but business users working across business units (as in the cases of Finance or Sales functions) might be stressed to work across two systems: SAP S/4HANA as well as the legacy system. As compared to other scenarios, it requires considerations of interim business processes if customers and business users are shared across the business units.

Customer Segment-Driven Deployment

In this approach, you deploy the SAP S/4HANA solution across specific customer segments at once. For example, if you are a retail company supplying to large customers such as Walmart and Costco, you can choose to deploy SAP S/4HANA for large customers at once, whereas another customer segment has to interact via the legacy system. Benefits of this approach include minimized customer impact with controlled data conversion activities. It is hard, though, for the business users from central functions such as Finance and Procurement, where they have to deal with multiple versions of the same process, depending on the customer with whom they are interacting. It increases operational complexity as well.

Apart from the scenarios just listed, the organization could also look for hybrid scenarios when specific functionalities are rolled out to the particular customer segments or business units. You can even group deployments with specific criteria; for example:

- The retirement of legacy systems to maximize business case, thus further simplifying cutovers.

- Businesses with the highest volume of transactions or revenue.

- Grouped by region or geographical location and cluster.

Arriving at a Deployment Strategy

Deployment scenarios are further customized to suit your organization. Multiple deployment approaches are then also ranked based on the essential criteria. Each criterion is then weighted. The overall score for a deployment option is arrived at by multiplying ranking with weight of criteria. Classification can be done as measured as low (1), medium (3), and high (5), depending on the applicability of criteria. More deliberate ranking mechanisms can be developed if you are looking for highly complex multiyear rollouts across multiple geographical or business units. Table 11-1 shows the different criteria with individual weightage scores, shown here only for the sake of the demonstration.

Table 11-1. *Ranking Deployment Approaches*

Scoring Criteria	Definition	Classification	Weightage
Timeline	Time taken for initial and subsequent releases	High	5
	Time taken for the program completion		
	Time taken for critical activities like data conversion or stabilization after go-live		
Implementation complexity	Dependencies with other projects	Medium	3
	Business disruption		
	Seasonality/business cycles		
	Impending mergers and acquisitions		
Change	Degree of organizational change	Low	1
	Number of users and sites affected		

(continued)

Table 11-1. (*continued*)

Scoring Criteria	Definition	Classification	Weightage
Process + technology	Scope of business functionality	Medium	3
	Level of data conversion effort for the master and transaction data		
Cost–benefit	Cost of the program	High	5
	Required resources in-house or contracted along with necessary skills		
	Licensing/infrastructure costs		
	Severance costs if any		
	Time to derive benefits and capabilities		
Interim processes	Number of standard/ nonstandard integrations to be built, along with the temporary processes	Medium	3
	Dual systems/retrofit management		
	Coexistence of systems as well as organizations, project and support		

Once done, it is easier to rank them by their scores, thus short-listing preferred options, as shown in the illustrative ranking of deployment options in Table 11-2. I have used a ranking system of 1 = least favorable, 3 = average, and 5 = preferred. You can generate your ranking system and multiply with weightage of specific factors to obtain scores.

In the example shown in Table 11-2, the big-bang deployment option seems to be a clear winner with the highest score.

Table 11-2. Evaluating Deployment Options

Scoring Criteria	weightage	Deployment Scenario Score				
		Value/Functionality Based	Big-Bang	Geography Driven	Business Unit Driven	Customer Segment Driven
Timeline	5	3	5	1	1	1
Implementation complexity	3	5	3	3	3	3
Change	1	3	3	3	1	3
Process + technology	3	5	3	3	5	5
Cost–benefit	5	3	5	5	1	1
Interim processes	3	1	5	3	3	1
Sum Total (Weightage x Score)		66	86	60	44	40

You can further fine-tune an SAP S/4HANA deployment strategy by applying additional levers as follows.

- *Simultaneous country roll-outs:* You increase the number of countries that can be deployed at the same time.

- *Concurrent deployment waves:* You increase the number of deployments running in parallel. This is a preferred strategy, especially for Central Finance implementations, although it is more expensive due to the additional resources required to facilitate other waves.

- *Standardized template:* A standard generic template is configured and deployed to select individual countries, thus minimizing the number of country-specific requirements.

- *In-scope countries or sites:* This reduces the number of countries or sites in scope for the project and focuses on the high-value countries in terms of overall revenue or transaction volume.

Governance Strategy

No matter how big or small your SAP S/4HANA implementation is, you should still consider proper program governance rather than routine project management that you have for any IT project. The program is a collection of diverse projects, whereas the IT project often manages a similar set of requirements or projects. During the SAP S/4HANA implementation, you work on multiple small projects making up the component, such as UI (Fiori), analytics, data conversion, change management, and so on. All these subprojects eventually contribute to the success of the SAP S/4HANA program, but they are often individually managed by respective workstream leads, reporting to overall program leadership.

Program governance during the SAP S/4HANA implementation follows a three-layer strategy.

- Operational (global and regional project teams)

    - The bottom layer is the operational support layer covering functions such as business and IT user support and back office auditing.

    - Teams in this layer focus on day-to-day operations of maintenance and delivery of solutions. They participate in project design workshops and provide requirements, manage third parties, provide security requirements and guidelines, implement critical decisions, and provide operational insights; they also lead local communications efforts and manage roll-outs.

- Tactical (global and regional project management)

    - The middle layer is the transformation and change management layer.

    - Teams in this layer focus on program management at the operational level, confirming that comprehensive release plans and budgets are defined, and resources have been garnered to deliver the agreed-on program objectives. They are responsible for tracking the various initiatives within your SAP S/4HANA program to make sure that they are delivered on schedule and on budget.

- This layer covers governance aspects related to stakeholder management, policy, and process optimization, and is generally responsible for executing the SAP S/4HANA deployment strategy.

- Strategic (global joint review board) or steering committee

  - The top layer is the system implementation layer. It covers solution design, template governance, and change control management.

  - A joint governance structure of critical leadership and stakeholders is established to confirm the program is achieving the overall business objectives and delivering the agreed-on value. It provides direction, review, and sign-off on crucial deliverables, engaging stakeholders as needed.

  - This layer is responsible for making sure the SAP S/4HANA business case is delivered, the business value is generated, and the associated costs are minimized during the implementation.

Once you finalize the project governance model, overall project organization can be drawn indicating various teams and their roles and responsibilities. Figure 11-1 shows a representative organization chart for an SAP S/4HANA project.

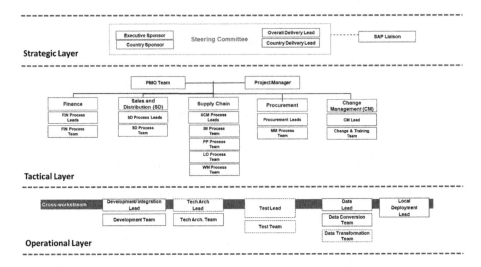

Figure 11-1. *Representative organization chart for an SAP S/4HANA project*

- This organization chart operates with the three-layer structure discussed earlier. The steering committee is at the top, made up of the project sponsors and delivery leads. It is supported by executive sponsors as well as SAP liaison members. This group monitors project health in terms of financials and deliverables and provides strategic direction to the project.

- It is followed by the tactical layer of the project management organization (PMO) function made up of individual project managers and support teams for pricing and reporting. This group feeds key project details to the steering committee to help them make better decisions. They also provide tactical coverage and work with operational project teams to manage SAP S/4HANA deployments.

- The operation project team is made up of teams working across the workstreams such as development, integration, data, testing, and deployment and cutover management. Operational teams handle the day-to-day project, run workshops, build deliverables, and arrange sign-offs. They feed project-related data to the tactical teams for generating insights related to project health.

Table 11-3 shows the vital roles and activities they conduct during the SAP S/4HANA implementation.

Table 11-3. *Key Roles and Their Activities*

Key Roles	Activities
Delivery lead/ steering committee	Provides execute-level oversight and sets overall SAP S/4HANA program direction. Accountable for the delivery of the project. Acts as a liaison between IT and business teams and helps manage relationships with stakeholders.
Project manager	Supports project planning, status reporting, and risk management. Also manages scope changes and handles various integration topics between teams.
PMO team	Provides administrative support to maintaining project plans, deliverable tracking, change control process, status reporting, risk and issues management and action management, resource management (onboarding, offboarding), and project financial management.
Process lead	Leads process design to ensure SAP S/4HANA capabilities and business requirements match. Leads testing as well as data conversion activities for process area.

(*continued*)

Table 11-3. (*continued*)

Key Roles	Activities
Process team	Helps with detailed functional design, configuration, and testing of the business requirements. Works with development teams on customizations.
Change management lead	Develops a change management approach, stakeholder management, change impact assessments, and communications (internal and external).
Change and training team	Develops training plan, and creates and delivers training materials to trainers using a train the trainer approach. Produces detailed change management deliverables.
Development or integration lead	Leads technical or integration design and ensures the integrity of interfaces between SAP S/4HANA and other systems. Leads development activities in line with development standards.
Development team	Helps with the development of RICEFWs. Works with process team for testing and defect fixing.
Technical architecture lead	Manages SAP S/4HANA hardware, software, networking, and environments. Helps to develop technical architecture strategy including sizing, archiving, and datacenter considerations. Leads the SAP S/4HANA migration effort.
Technical architecture team	Handles day-to-day operations. Manages SAP S/4HANA environments and related networking and infrastructure issues. Supports activation of Fiori UI and standard Fiori applications.
Security team	Helps design, build, and implement application and network security.
Test lead	Leads multiple test cycles, including regression, performance testing, SIT, and UAT.

(*continued*)

Table 11-3. (*continued*)

Key Roles	Activities
Test team	Develops test scripts and scenarios. Participates in multiple cycles of testing.
Data lead	Helps to develop and execute a data conversion strategy including cleansing, validation, extract, transformation, and load activities. Leads to data conversion and transformation effort.
Data conversion team	Conducts data conversions in SAP S/4HANA environments. Help to design and build data conversion objects and test them via multiple mock conversions.
Data transformation team	Conducts data transformations via SAP Data Services/IS or any other data transformation tool. Helps to design and build data transformations and test them during multiple mock conversions.
Local deployment lead	Leads local in-country deployments. Liaises with local stakeholders and project teams. Leads local change management effort.

CHAPTER 12

Building a Business Case for S/4HANA

So far, we have discussed various components involved in the SAP S/4HANA implementation. During the planning phase, each of these components goes through an individual assessment. Such an assessment helps to determine the scope of each component and enables you to identify the costs associated with it. Business case evaluation is run in parallel with the assessment workshops. It uses inputs from these workshops to identify opportunities for improvements.

Business Case Evaluation Exercise

The following are the objectives of the business case evaluation exercise.

- Determine strategic fit to SAP S/4HANA.

  - How will SAP S/4HANA capabilities enable our business and operating strategy?

  - What is the degree of impact across the organization?

  - How will SAP S/4HANA contribute to our strategy and financial plans?

© Sanket Kulkarni 2019
S. Kulkarni, *Implementing SAP S/4HANA*, https://doi.org/10.1007/978-1-4842-4520-0_12

- Calculate value realized by various SAP S/4HANA opportunities.

    - How much can SAP S/4HANA help us improve our baseline performance?

    - Will the program pay for itself, and what ROI can we expect based on the funding required?

- Outline SAP S/4HANA deployment approach.

    - How do we execute SAP S/4HANA deployments?

    - Are there any in-flight initiatives that can potentially affect SAP S/4HANA implementation?

- Ensure business buy-in by prioritizing SAP S/4HANA initiatives that create the highest value.

    - Who will sponsor or endorse the program?

    - Where are our champions and change agents?

    - Is SAP S/4HANA implementation worth doing? Is it worth doing now?

Business case discussions are embedded in the workshops you usually run for process and technology components in SAP S/4HANA. Here are the steps involved in the business case evaluation.

1. It begins with a visioning workshop. Strategic objectives are laid out and fit of SAP S/4HANA in helping achieve those objectives is discussed at length.

    a. For example, you start by outlining strategic objectives such as attaining the leadership position in your industry or charting a path of business growth and profit. The value proposition of SAP

S/4HANA is then described in terms of how it can help you simplify business processes, modernize ERP, and so on.

2. Multiple process workshops are run to identify the requirements and capabilities of SAP S/4HANA. Generally, the focus is set on best practices and minimizing customizations.

    a. For example, the SAP S/4HANA Sales and Distribution capability might help you improve sales productivity or help you roll out promotions and pricing intelligently.

3. Key value opportunities are identified for each process area. Detailed discussions are held to set out as-is and to-be processes specifically for each opportunity.

    a. For example, you might want to improve inventory turns for your organization. Inventory turn is calculated as the cost of goods sold for the year divided by the average value of month-end finished goods inventory for the most recently completed fiscal year. Let us assume that your current inventory turn is 2.

    b. SAP S/4HANA can help you improve inventory turns in the following ways:

        i. Enhancing visibility of inventory with integrated intercompany stock transfer order planning and processes.

        ii. Implementing efficient quality management processing and inventory control functionalities.

       iii. Having real-time reporting with Embedded Analytics.

4. Business benefits are calculated in common currency. Here the focus is on data-driven analysis rather than relying on general information. Industry-level benchmarks are used for comparison and assess the potential for value generation.

    a. Industry-level benchmarks are sought either from the American Productivity and Quality Center (APQC) or SAP Value Lifecycle Manager.

    b. For example, APQC says that the typical inventory turns value for your industry is 3. So, by implementing the SAP S/4HANA functionalities listed earlier, you can improve your inventory turns to 3, thus reducing the cost of goods sold (inventory) by $10 million.

    c. The business benefit of value lever by implementing SAP S/4HANA is thus $10 million.

5. Such information is then adjusted for qualitative factors selectively. Qualitative factors often involve business and regulatory risks, readiness for change, process and technology maturity, and scalability considerations.

6. Budgets and investments needed for each SAP S/4HANA opportunity are calculated. Governance and deployment strategies are finalized. Capital expenses (CAPEX) and operational expenses (OPEX) are calculated based on resourcing, licensing, and infrastructure costs.

7. Finally, prioritization of the SAP S/4HANA
    opportunities is done by development of the matrix
    showcasing benefits vs. investments. Preferred
    opportunities for implementation are the ones that
    provide higher benefits at lower investments.

Value Drivers

Value drivers are the factors that generate value for your organization
either by increasing revenue or reducing costs or improving productivity
in some cases. While developing a business case for SAP S/4HANA,
you should identify value drivers best suited for the digital business
transformation in your respective industry.

Such value levers can be categorized across three areas.

- They help you grow revenues by:

    - Providing better process support, thus increasing
      process efficiency.

    - Introducing new business capabilities through
      incremental changes to functionality.

    - Enabling better decision quality by making relevant
      information readily available.

- They optimize costs by:

    - Reducing end-to-end transaction time.

    - Reducing the transaction errors, and thus reducing
      rework involved.

    - Helping streamline the processes based on instant
      insights (analytics).

- They increase the efficiency of your organization by:

  - Reducing FTEs required for executing day-to-day transactions and allocating more time for other (value-added) activities.

  - Providing ubiquitous access to information via Fiori apps.

Table 12-1 demonstrates value drivers relevant for an SAP S/4HANA implementation.

Table 12-1. *Value Drivers*

Objectives	Business Goals	Value Drivers
Grow revenues	Acquire and retain customers	Acquire new customers
		Improve customer engagement
		Drive customer loyalty
		Increase customer satisfaction
		Offer personalized services
	Improve product mix/ pricing	Optimize prices
		Better demand forecasting
	Improve sales process	Better promotions planning
		Better merchandising and assortment planning
		Better collection management

(*continued*)

Table 12-1. (*continued*)

Objectives	Business Goals	Value Drivers
Optimize costs	Reduce operations costs, thus improving operations yield	Reduce cost of goods sold (COGS)
		Reduce technology costs
		Optimize personnel costs
Increase efficiency	Better resource management	Better cash flow management
		Improve working capital

Each of these value drivers is further associated with value levers. Value levers are KPIs or business metrics that you use to measure value drivers. These value levers are useful to measure benefits of SAP S/4HANA implementation. Benefits are calculated by comparing as-is and to-be values. Table 12-2 displays a sample list of value levers across the process areas.

Table 12-2. *Value Levers*

Process Teams	Value Levers
Sales and distribution	COGS — Inventories
	Selling, general, and administrative expenses (SG&A) —Administrative costs
	SG&A — Technology costs
	Revenue — Operating margin
	Working capital — Accounts receivable

(*continued*)

Table 12-2. (*continued*)

Process Teams	Value Levers
Materials management	COGS — Inventories
	COGS — Materials
	SG&A — Personnel
	Working capital — Inventories
Manufacturing	COGS — Materials
	COGS — Personnel
	SG&A — Personnel
Finance	SG&A — Personnel
Technology	SG&A — Technology costs

Let us take one example of a value driver and explain how business case benefits are visualized. Let's say you want to improve outstanding sales. You are looking at the business objective of growing revenues by improving sales processes. A key value driver applicable to outstanding sales is to have better collection management.

The value lever by which you monitor outstanding sales is working capital — accounts receivable (AR). You currently have $350 million of open AR items from the as-is analysis. It is turning out to be 45 days sales outstanding.

You first analyze why there is a higher amount of AR. You figure out that its due to these factors:

- The existing collection management tool is not integrated with SAP on a real-time basis and has limited features and capabilities.

- Real-time balance and payment position are not available, mainly due to delays in data load.

- Delays are also due to manual cash application, as the SWIFT Electronic Bank functionality is not used in some cases.

- The process lacks drill-down capability at the transactional level because collection agents have to go back to SAP if required.

Then, you determine that specific SAP S/4HANA capabilities like Financial Supply Chain Management (FSCM) with their collection and dispute management functionalities can add a lot of value as follows.

- Collection management is integrated with AR, enabling collection agents to get real-time information on account balances, cash collection, dispute cases, and so on.

- Collection agents have transaction visibility to see invoice details, and invoice copies can be sent directly over e-mail.

- Collection receivables are prioritized using work lists based on amount outstanding, risk category, disputes, and so on.

Then, you look for industry benchmarks like APQC and SAP Value Manager, which tell you that for your industry, average days sales outstanding (DSO) is 30 days. Therefore, a conservative estimate of benefits by implementing SAP FSCM best practices is around 15 DSP, which can be converted into AR benefits of $25 million.

SAP Value Lifecycle Manager

SAP Value Lifecycle Manager (VLM) can help you calculate the potential benefits based on the publicly available information and benchmark averages. Benchmarks in VLM are a result of the global benchmarking programs that SAP has run for more than 8,000 organizations. VLM inventory includes around 50 benchmarking surveys with more than 2,500 KPIs and more than 3,500 best practices.

It is also used to develop a detailed business case where cost and benefit data is captured to calculate your project ROI along with the payback period. The data and KPIs from the benchmark surveys and templates are projected as benefits in the business case.

In summary, SAP VLM is used for the following benefits:

- To identify and prioritize process improvement opportunities for SAP S/4HANA.

- To benchmark KPIs and best practices by process area or industry.

- To monitor your value realization throughout the project by continuous measurement of KPIs and process.

Cost Drivers

Cost drivers help you understand the cost of SAP S/4HANA implementation. To arrive at the cost of your SAP S/4HANA program, you should have a clear understanding of various SAP S/4HANA components and the effort needed to implement them.

During the planning phase, effort is arrived at by defining the scope up front and setting up estimation guidelines. In principle, your estimation guidelines for each scope area are developed in two ways. It can be either parameter-driven or FTE-driven.

Table 12-3 provides initial guidance based on the SAP S/4HANA components discussed in the earlier chapters. The more elaborate estimation guidelines you have, the more you develop an understanding of work delivered in each area, and thus have more assurance of providing the work as planned.

Table 12-3. *Estimation Guidelines*

Scope Area	Estimation Guideline	Estimation Parameters	Considerations
Process/functional effort	Mainly parameter-driven augmented by FTEs	Number of business processes, number of functional/configuration specifications	Consider adding additional FTE effort to account for template governance, training delivery, deployment, and solution architecture
Development effort	Parameter-driven	RICEFW list with complexities for Greenfield or number of objects to be remediated in case of Brownfield implementation	Consider adding additional FTE effort for integration/development architect, middleware, or legacy-end development
Data effort	Parameter-driven	Number of conversion objects, number of mock conversions, volume of data	Consider additional FTEs around data cleansing, verification, and dress-rehearsal activities

(*continued*)

Table 12-3. (*continued*)

Scope Area	Estimation Guideline	Estimation Parameters	Considerations
Testing effort	Parameter-driven	Number of assembly/regression/performance/UAT test scripts	Consider additional FTEs for test automation. Consider extra effort for HA/DR testing, test management, and defect remediation by functional and development teams
Technical architecture effort	FTE-driven	Application stack, number of environments, number of roles (single/composite) across applications, GRC considerations	Allocate FTEs for BASIS/security over the deployment roadmap
Organization change management effort	FTE-driven	Number of users/superusers, locations for training, number of processes covered in the training materials, simulations, user instructions, language considerations	Consider separate training development FTEs augmented by functional interlock effort, as functional FTEs will drive training content

Fiori effort	FTE-driven	Number of Fiori apps to be enabled or customized	Fiori app enablement effort is often minimal, though customization of Fiori apps will warrant additional FTEs in terms of UI design and testing
Embedded Analytics effort	FTE-driven	Number of reports: the number of Fiori Analytical apps, number of integrations or extractions and customization of CDS views	Consider additional FTEs for extensive testing of the reports
Governance and deployment effort	FTE-driven	Number of operating locations (hub), rollouts, governance model	Consider adding FTEs around cutover or country localization as well as program leadership

Clearly defined scope and estimation guidelines help you arrive at the effort for all of the listed scope areas. Then, such effort is mapped to the SAP S/4HANA deployment roadmap developed during the governance and deployment strategy. Once assigned, it gives you useful guidance in terms of resources required with associated skills. For example, you like to carry program governance for the entire duration of the program. Thus, it is directly dependent on the months it takes to deploy SAP S/4HANA. On the other hand, you decide to conduct training activities close to go-live.

Staffing effort is then multiplied with a rate card (internal or IT vendors) based on the effort allocation across the various parties involved in the project. It helps to arrive at the labor cost of your SAP S/4HANA program. You can further allocate some portion of it as CAPEX or OPEX, depending on the business rules. SAP S/4HANA implementation costs can be further optimized by using either scope or deliver levers.

Scope Levers

Scope levers aim for reduction or optimization of the scope for an SAP S/4HANA component. Scope levers can be identified by asking the following questions.

- Are you including anything that can be excluded? For example, can analytics strategy be separated and tackled later once SAP S/4HANA is stabilized?

- Are you building a "luxury car" when a "family sedan" will do?

  - A common trap while building a business case for SAP S/4HANA is to get lured into all the promises and target "moon landing" on the first go. Having a realistic handle on your organization's appetite for change often helps.

- Can you reduce overall scope by using best practices, thus reducing the plumbing and replumbing into the legacy, thus reducing RICEFWs, and associated testing effort?

Delivery Levers

Delivery levers focus on ways to execute the project efficiently while targeting lower costs. They are identified by asking the following questions.

- Can you move more work offshore by working with IT partners, thus reducing overall labor costs while expending the same effort?

  - You might have to consider additional project management and coordination effort, although it is often offset by the savings you get from moving work offshore.

- Can you consider an alliance or teaming partner who can deliver one or more components at a lower overall cost, reserving high value-added components to yourself?

Additional Considerations

A sample baseline for costing details would be useful to understand the overall cost. You should include a simple implementation costing. Once you have optimized SAP S/4HANA implementation costs by pulling scope and delivery levers, here are some additional considerations to arrive at overall SAP S/4HANA program costs:

- Buffer (contingency) costs if assumptions behind baseline cost numbers change slightly.

- Additional decommissioning costs.

  - You should offset it by reduced infrastructure and organizational resources.

- Licensing costs for the SAP S/4HANA application stack.

- Software and hardware costs.

- Infrastructure costs for SAP S/4HANA application stack, whether its cloud or on-premise.

- Severance costs if SAP S/4HANA implementation is helping you to reduce resources involved in managing the existing monolith legacy system.

- Expenses (one-time or recurring), including travel and expenses for project teams and the cost of the necessary infrastructure to hold workshops during the projects.

- Participation variance in terms of how SAP S/4HANA implementation effort is distributed between you and IT vendors.

- Forex (FX) impact if you are planning rollouts in multiple countries, and thus will spend on the resources in different currencies than the base currency used to build a business case.

  - In this case, additional Forex contingency should be baked into the SAP S/4HANA program costs.

- Your resourcing costs rise in line with inflation index (often termed cost-of-living adjustment [COLA]) as monitored by Aon-Hewitt. Inflation index varies by locations where resources are located. If you are running a multiyear program across multiple global locations, you should consider COLA impact up front.

- Discounts, including volume discounts or discounts instead of an up-front payment, often part of the agreements with your IT vendors.

- Warranties, as some functionalities might require extended hypercare support.

  - For example, SAP S/4HANA Finance (or even Central Finance) implementations require period-end closing (or even quarter-end in some cases) as valid sign-off considerations. This means that you need to carry your project team longer than expected, affecting program costs.

In summary, here are the various cost elements considered during SAP S/4HANA implementation.

- Contingency

  - Percent applied to the resourcing costs.

- Nonlabor

  - License fee one time.

  - Software maintenance fees year-on-year.

  - Infrastructure and cloud costs.

  - Peripherals costs (printers, scanners, etc.).

- Labor

  - Internal labor costs mapped to internal rates.

  - Internal labor travel expenses.

  - External (third-party) labor costs mapped to their rates.

  - External labor travel expenses.

- Internal costs for legacy adjustments, data cleansing, and decommissioning.

- Severance costs.

- Maintenance costs for application and infrastructure.

Building a Business Case

Once you have cost as well as value drivers identified and related cost–benefit numbers are worked out, you can group value drivers (SAP S/4HANA opportunities) as individual initiatives; for example, Analytics, Master Data Governance, Supply Chain Improvement, and so on. These initiatives are then run via qualitative analysis. Such an analysis validates each SAP S/4HANA initiative via benefits, cost, and risk filters. It is mainly assessing them against a range of questions as follows:

- Benefits

  - Do you want to standardize or harmonize global processes?

    - Standardization focuses on using SAP and industry best practices, whereas harmonization focuses on generating a common theme across all process variations. It also affects master data decisions and incurs additional costs to harmonize it.

  - How does future mergers and acquisitions activity affect priorities and associated benefits?

  - Do SAP S/4HANA processes fully reflect current and future business requirements?

  - Are new features of SAP S/4HANA critical to embark on a large-scale transformation?

- Risks

  - Is the priority to reduce business impact by distributing deployments over a longer timeline?

  - Is a delayed realization of SAP S/4HANA related benefits acceptable for each initiative?

  - Do you require individual rollout for different business units or functional areas? Is reducing change management efforts and scope preferred over a shorter project timeline? These and other related questions are covered while deciding the deployment strategy for SAP S/4HANA.

- Costs

  - Are business benefits significant enough to justify a more extended implementation project?

  - Is the business process change desired to justify a higher effort from business users during the implementation?

  - Is a higher operational cost acceptable to support many customizations? Or should you adopt standardized processes to reduce operational costs further?

Once such initiatives are passed through the filter of qualitative analysis, they are then plotted in a value realization matrix by having benefits due to value driver on one axis and cost drivers on another one. You therefore know the initiatives that can provide better "bang for the buck"—higher benefits at lower costs, thus better ROI. In drawing the SAP S/4HANA roadmap, such initiatives can then be fast-tracked to generate value faster, while keeping program costs under control.

Some initiatives, although very attractive, might not even make sense due to poor ROI because of higher costs and limited business benefits. You can postpone them in the SAP S/4HANA deployment plan or treat them as an innovation item until the core SAP S/4HANA functionality is built and stabilized. At a later point in time, you can revalidate the business case for those specific items to check whether it makes the business case for pursuing such items.

In summary, the deliverables of the business case evaluation exercise are as follows:

- A value realization matrix showcasing value drivers (benefits) vs. cost drivers (costs) analysis for each of the SAP S/4HANA initiatives.

- Prioritization of SAP S/4HANA initiatives with near-term, medium-term, and future-term categorization based on the value realization matrix.

- A revised deployment plan showcasing sequencing of various SAP S/4HANA initiatives.

- A finalized SAP S/4HANA transformation roadmap with details like timeline, resources, target architecture, and most important, ROI statistics. It also includes targets for value drivers based on to-be state, which is to be monitored throughout the program.

CHAPTER 13

Alternative S/4HANA Implementation Approaches

So far, we have discussed various components of implementing SAP S/4HANA with the On-Premise Edition in mind. Most of these aspects remain the same regardless of whether you are using a Greenfield or Brownfield implementation. Apart from implementing the On-Premise Edition, there are also alternative approaches to undertake the SAP S/4HANA journey.

If your processes are highly customized, and you do not want to rush to complete SAP S/4HANA functionality at once, a two-step approach of implementing Central Finance first, then going for the SAP S/4HANA full suite is worth considering. On the other hand, if you are seriously leaning toward standardization, follow best practices to a great extent, and keep customization minimal, SAP S/4HANA Cloud Edition can be an option.

So far, we have also discussed SAP S/4HANA Greenfield and Brownfield implementation approaches at length. Risks with Brownfield implementation are escalated with the requirement to migrate full-scale data to the production system at once. Organizations are looking to mitigate such data-related risks by converting configurations first and then migrating data in batches as per the rollout deployment schedule. Such an

© Sanket Kulkarni 2019
S. Kulkarni, *Implementing SAP S/4HANA*, https://doi.org/10.1007/978-1-4842-4520-0_13

approach is called Bluefield or shell conversion. We discuss these three alternate approaches—Central Finance, SAP S/4HANA Cloud Edition, and Bluefield implementation—in the sections that follow.

Central Finance

Central Finance is often used as an intermediate path to SAP S/4HANA so that it does not burden you with moving the entire back-end ERP infrastructure while still giving you a flavor for the innovations in SAP S/4HANA such as Universal Journal or faster financial reporting. For customers having a multi-ERP landscape or highly customized ERP system, the transition to SAP S/4HANA is often scary. The obvious pain point for having such a landscape is fragmented or time-lagged financial and management reporting. Central Finance addresses it by separating the financial reporting layer from the transaction layer. Transactions still happen in the back-end ERP system, which might or might not be on SAP S/4HANA. The reporting layer is built into the SAP S/4HANA system with replications created from the back-end ERPs to regularly feed financial data. Apart from building integrations with SAP S/4HANA Finance, this approach does not need you to make any changes to the back-end ERPs.

Central Finance, being a nondisruptive option to implement SAP S/4HANA, starts with establishing a single source of truth—financial reporting based on Universal Journal entries across the organization. Accounting documents from the back-end ERP systems with different data models are replicated in real time to Central Finance with a harmonized data model. Please note that harmonization of data is critical for any Central Finance implementation. As expected, it is the one that often takes the most time and effort up front and cannot be fast-tracked as such.

Source systems continue to be the leading systems for any operational processes. The impact on source systems is limited to the installation of notes, additional tables in the source system that need to be cleared periodically, and possible process changes to support the standard reporting structure. Central Finance enables instant central reporting on the line item level based on the standard reporting structure, called SAP Code Block or Universal Journal.

Mapping of different accounting entities (e.g., G/L accounts, profit centers, cost centers) is then defined between each source ERP system and the Central Finance system. During the replication process, finance and controlling (FICO) documents from each source ERP system are then mapped to Universal Journal entries.

Universal Journal

In pre-SAP S/4HANA days, different tables were used to capture financial data related to the general ledger, profitability, management accounting, asset accounting, and material ledger. In the new Central Finance system, you have a single line item table, ACDOCA, with details from all the applications just listed.

Universal Journal ensures that data is stored only once, and no replication is needed again by design. That is why it is called a single source of truth. It helps with instant reporting and faster period-end closing in the SAP S/4HANA system.

Transaction data harmonization is done via mapping layer SLT, and master data harmonization is done via existing SAP Master Data Governance (MDG) tool. Use of SAP MDG is optional, as there are other ways to sync master data from the legacy ERP to the Central Finance system.

As shown in Figure 13-1, the Universal Journal entry is made after mapping financial documents from the source system to the Central Finance system.

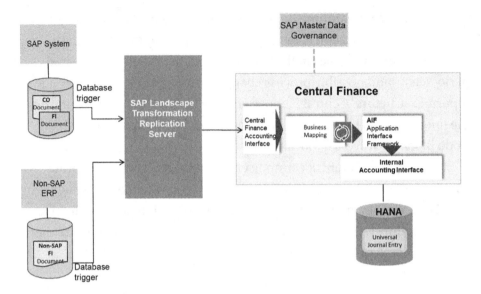

Figure 13-1. *Central Finance architecture*

You should opt for Central Finance under these conditions:

- You have heterogeneous data structures and a diverse system landscape across the enterprise.

- Period-end closing is often delayed and fraught with issues that have to be tackled with manual fixes every time.

- You want to have a real-time financial planning and reporting solution.

- You have done or are in the process of doing acquisitions and expansions and struggle to integrate a slew of systems that have been added to your landscape.

- It takes time to double-click for details in financial and management reporting, as you would then have to manually go to the source and work out bottom-up numbers.

- Your ERP landscape is not just SAP, but non-SAP as well, leading to issues with integration and data mapping.

Implementation Approach

Central Finance implementations often follow a multistep approach by introducing different functionalities at different points in time. It is done to ensure that the foundation for an SAP code block (Universal Journal) is stabilized before adding advanced functionalities like reporting and consolidation.

1. You introduce core functionalities such as MDG integration, necessary financial document reconciliation, and standard corporate management reporting.

2. Then, you activate legal and statutory reporting based on the available data. Tax reporting and fraud prevention also follow later.

3. You enable functionalities relevant to your financial shared services function such as central payables and receivables, cash management, credit management, and so on.

4. Planning, budgeting, and real-time consolidation follow once all previous steps are completed, and the replication mechanism is stabilized and error free.

Let us next discuss various scope areas involved in the Central Finance implementation.

Functional Scope

Defining the target data model is key to successful implementation. The target data model can be envisaged as a single data entity with all necessary financial details such as account, company code, order, document type, WBS (Work Breakdown Structure), profit center, trading partner, and so on. As these details come from single- or multiple-source ERP systems, relevant mapping rules are required to be configured. Gaps between source ERP data and the target SAP S/4HANA data model are identified. One of the options to address such differences is to manage it at the source ERP level by developing customizations.

Because target data model complexity (in terms of the number of objects in scope and the number of records per object) along with the degree of process and data harmonization often drive the implementation schedule, conscious effort is made to minimize customizations and address data-related issues at the source.

Development Scope

Gaps between source ERP and Central Finance data structures are addressed by developing additional customizations via business add-ins (BADI). There is also development effort required at source systems for mapping adjustments if any. Various types of mapping rules (key, value, or cost object) are developed and tested for the replication of the financial data coming from back-end ERP systems.

- Value mapping is used when codes used in master data attributes (company code, country code, etc.) are different between systems.

- Key mapping is used when the primary key of an object (customer ID, material ID, etc.) is different in various systems.

- Cost object mapping allows mapping cost objects (internal order, production order, etc.) in the source system to cost objects in the SAP S/4HANA Central Finance system.

Development effort is also expected on SAP MDG for mapping rules, if necessary, via BADIs.

Data Scope

Master data and transaction data replication into the Central Finance system is a primary activity during the project. A lot of effort is spent on setting and refining mapping rules and testing data replication iteratively. Each replication cycle throws up some data error that is fixed via data cleansing or updating of mapping rules. Once set, reloading of data is done until replication is completed successfully.

Testing Scope

Testing scope in the Central Finance project is about replication of master and transaction data. Performance testing of the intermediate SLT layer is critical, as near real-time updates on many financial documents are expected to consume a lot of system resources. Replication errors are tested via multiple loads until there is a certain degree of confidence built. Mapping rules are refined further by functional and development teams based on replication errors. They are thoroughly tested again for validation.

Each test cycle is comprised of a series of steps starting with master data migration, followed by cost object load, MDG mapping, and FICO document posting, concluding with validation and spot checks for real-time replications.

Technical Architecture

Central Finance is often a separate instance from SAP S/4HANA if you are looking for a two-tier architecture. It has to be licensed separately as well. It is available only on SAP S/4HANA On-Premise Edition hosted in a private cloud or client infrastructure. Setting up of the SLT layer for interfacing with the back-end ERP system and monitoring replication performance is an important activity from the technical architecture side.

Organizational Change Management

Central Finance is often limited to a small number of users in the Finance function, so change management or training effort is often minimal.

Fiori

Central Finance uses standard analytical apps available in the Fiori repository. Enablement of standard Fiori apps is enough for reporting requirements in most cases.

Embedded Analytics

Embedded Analytics capabilities in Central Finance are limited to analytical apps available in the Fiori dashboard.

S/4HANA Cloud

In February 2017, SAP launched a public cloud edition of the SAP S/4HANA Suite. SAP S/4HANA Cloud (S4HC) Edition offers the option to SAP customers to move their ERP landscape to the cloud. This SaaS-based ERP product covers all key business processes such as finance and logistics. As for any SaaS-based product, SAP S/4HANA Cloud Edition offers lower total cost of ownership (TCO) and is easy to scale and to upgrade.

There are two options for implementing S/4HANA Cloud Edition.

- SAP S/4HANA Cloud (S4HC) refers to the multitenant solution, a full SaaS model with a Fiori front end and four quarterly upgrades per year. It is hosted on a public cloud infrastructure managed by SAP.

  - It has a limited set of business processes and country localizations available. Hence it is prudent to validate it beforehand specifically for your industry.

- SAP S/4HANA Cloud single-tenant is a private cloud installation of Enterprise Management, with cloud hosting managed by SAP and two upgrades every year.

  - If you are not ready for a multitenant SaaS ERP system, the single tenant version is worth considering. The single-tenant version was introduced in 2018 to provide an alternative to the multitenant option, providing the full business process and global localizations as SAP S/4HANA On-Premise in the cloud.

  - It follows business processes modeled around SAP best practices. Integration with other SAP and non-SAP systems is standardized using whitelisted APIs published in the SAP API Hub.

The degree of customization allowed either for multitenant or singletenant products is low. That is the critical difference with the SAP S/4HANA On-Premise Edition. Degree of customization required is a crucial decision factor in whether to use On-Premise or Cloud Editions. S4HC is the preferred choice for businesses where differentiation does not play a big part, and a high degree of standardization can help. For example, if you are a midsized software services company, S4HC might be the right choice, as it comes with preconfigured best practices, thus helping you reduce the TCO.

As compared to the S4HC multitenant model, the single-tenant model includes the full functionality of the SAP S/4HANA On-Premise Edition, but it is offered as an SaaS model. It is a complete solution in the cloud with the same feature, industry, and language support as the on-premise software, but with SAP-managed infrastructure and upgrades.

SAP sets several constraints on single-tenant installations called the Five Golden Rules to allow for biannual upgrades and eventual compatibility with the multitenant edition. However, there is no transition roadmap available from SAP S/4HANA On-Premise Edition to SAP S/4HANA Cloud Edition or S4HC single tenant to S4HC multitenant scenarios now.

Here are Fhe five Golden Rules for implementation of the S4HC single-tenant edition.

- Foster cloud mindset and adherence to fit-to-standard approach around SAP best practices.

- Model business processes around S4HC best practices and follow SAP Activate guidelines. Identified gaps in the business processes are evaluated for extensions.

- Develop cloud-like integrations

  - Use public whitelisted APIs from SAP API Hub.

  - No native access to nonpublic API.

- Develop cloud-like extensions

  - Develop customer extensions in a side-by-side approach using the SAP Cloud Platform or in-app development.

  - No source code modification allowed.

- Manage deviations carefully, as periodic upgrades might affect them, and thus have to be tested thoroughly again.

Any SAP S/4HANA Cloud implementation *comes with three system landscapes:* development, QA, and production. You begin with the starter and QA environment. As you move toward the deployment phase, the development environment is decommissioned. QA and production environments are retained and used for any further changes and test requirements.

Note that upgrades are mandatory under this model and the software is upgraded directly in your QA instance. Per SAP, you get about two weeks to complete testing before upgrades are moved to the production instance. Because extensions are done in SAP Cloud Platform and developed within extensibility guidelines, the impact to your customizations due to the periodic upgrades is often minimal.

Implementation Considerations

Let us understand the different scope areas involved in the SAP S/4HANA Cloud implementation.

Functional Scope

You compare the functional requirements against what is available in the best practices and identify gaps, if any. The focus is on fitting those gaps into the back-to-standard scenario rather than leaving them open for further extensions. Conference room pilots using the starter system helps as you assess each functional area and do an in-depth assessment.

Development Scope

Customizations, if necessary, are tracked and tested very carefully for potential impact on the best practices scenarios. Because you eventually have periodic upgrades as part of your licensing arrangement with SAP, it is in your best interest to reduce the level of customization. Extensions are developed side-by-side in the SAP Cloud Platform, which is often a separate instance than your core SAP S/4HANA cloud instance. Such offsite developments protect your core S4HC environment during upgrades.

Data Scope

SAP has provided standard data upload programs and templates that are used to kick-start data conversion. Although extraction or transformation happens entirely outside the S4HC system, the data conversion process is highly simplified due to prebuilt data migration tools.

Testing Scope

The QA environment of S4HC is used as a test laboratory. Activate methodology is applied to a great extent to manage the entire test effort. Best practices scenarios come with test documents and scenarios that are modified to accommodate extensions, if any. Test scope is assumed to be minimal, limited to customizations and their impact on the end-to-end scenarios. During the periodic upgrades, automatic regression testing is executed in the QA environment once extensions are thoroughly tested.

Technical Architecture

Technical architecture is straightforward as compared to the S/4HANA On-Premise Edition. Choice of cloud vendors can be worked out with SAP, and environments are provisioned quickly. Scaling of the environment is also easy, as your data volume and users ramp up in the production environment.

SAP S4HC is designed to operate out of single datacenter locations. Thus disaster recovery-based SLAs are often not available. If you choose a multidatacenter scenario (plausible only in a single-tenant architecture), SAP also has provisions to accommodate standard disaster recovery arrangements with specific SLAs.

Organizational Change Management

OCM effort is considerable as compared to an on-premise project. Because you are driving your processes toward back-to-standard, you spend a lot of effort on stakeholder buy-ins. You also need to train end users to let go of old customized processes and adopt SAP best practices. You can use existing Activate or best practices documents to kick-start your training effort. If you have a consensus-driven organization, then you will need to invest a lot of effort at the beginning of the project to secure necessary buy-ins from the stakeholders.

Fiori

Preenabled in SAP S/4HANA Cloud, FIORI apps can be adapted based on SAP best practices. Customization of the Fiori apps is discouraged.

Embedded Analytics

Embedded Analytics capabilities in S4HC are limited to the Analytical Apps in the Fiori dashboard.

Bluefield Implementation

Bluefield implementation approach provides the best of both Greenfield and Brownfield implementations.

A Greenfield approach is suitable when you are reengineering existing processes and adopting SAP best practices as feasible. The problem with this approach is that it takes a long time to implement and requires more effort, making it more costly to implement.

The Brownfield approach is suitable when you are migrating an old SAP ERP system to SAP S/4HANA. No new capabilities are introduced. Business processes run the same as they did in the legacy SAP ERP system. The problem with this approach is that you do not get enough value from moving SAP S/4HANA, as old processes, no matter how customized and antiquated they are, continue to run as usual. Data migration also happens in big-bang fashion, and thus takes a long time to execute.

Most organizations approach SAP S/4HANA implementation with three simple premises:

- Adopt SAP best practices whenever possible, while limiting drastic changes in already streamlined business processes.

- Reduce data conversion effort and time associated with it. Reduce risks of data conversion by batching or migrating data selectively.

- Reduce impacts on internal and external stakeholders by reducing interface and design changes.

A Bluefield approach tries to achieve these objectives by following a four-step process.

1. SAP S/4HANA assessment is done across all scope areas, as discussed in earlier chapters. System landscape, data, and process requirements are finalized.

2. The SAP S/4HANA shell is created using the SAP conversion process, which helps to migrate from SAP ERP to SAP S/4HANA. Custom code

remediation and mandatory process simplification steps are completed. Now, you have an empty SAP S/4HANA shell with all the necessary configuration but without master and transactional data. This is also called an S/4HANA golden instance.

3. You create SAP S/4HANA project environments (Development, QA, Production) using a system copy of the S/4HANA golden instance.

4. Selective data migration is done using the Data Migration cockpit or SAP Data Services. If you are having a series of rollouts as part of the SAP S/4HANA deployment strategy, data selected is relevant only for current deployment (organizational entities). Such selection reduces the overall data migration scope, and thus improves the time taken.

Some organization also follow a near-zero-downtime (NZDT) process to improve data conversion time during cutover. With NZDT, the production system continues to run while the data conversion happens. It replicates the data changes at frequent intervals, instead of requiring a full data snapshot once production systems are down. Because the primary data replication is done during uptime, only a small data set is required to load during downtime, which happens very fast.

Conclusion

There are four variants of SAP S/4HANA to choose from when you are about to embark on the SAP S/4HANA journey. There are a variety of factors that drive the decision about the right SAP S/4HANA version fit for you. You can refer to Table 13-1 to understand more about the factors involved in decision making among SAP S/4HANA variants.

Table 13-1. *Factors Involved in Choosing the Right SAP S/4HANA Variants*

	SAP S/4HANA Cloud	SAP S/4HANA Cloud Single-Tenant	SAP S/4HANA Private Cloud	SAP S/4HANA On-Premise
Overview	Multitenant ERP solution with a focus on the best practices and minimal customizations. Hosted and managed by SAP.	Single-tenant ERP solution with on-premise functionalities such as configuration and extended scope of customization. Hosted and managed by SAP.	Full-fledged ERP solution with on-premise functionalities such as configuration and extended customizations. Licensed by SAP but can be hosted on any cloud vendor.	Full-fledged ERP solution with on-premise functionalities such as configuration and extended customizations. Licensed by SAP, hosted on customer infrastructure.
License	Packaged. One monthly payment covers everything from infrastructure, software support, and daily backup, to upgrades.	Packaged. The monthly payment covers infrastructure, software support, daily backup, and upgrades. Cost is higher than multitenant, as the full "on-premise" software is licensed.	Customer purchases an SAP license separately from hosting. The cloud vendor provides infrastructure and operating system license.	License fee enables the company to own the software. Up-front purchase with annual maintenance.

Support and maintenance	SAP provides system support and maintenance with scheduled upgrades every quarter.	Three environments included, and initial Fiori activation included. Transports managed by client/partner. System refreshes and client copies are possible for an extra cost.	The cloud service provider maintains all IT infrastructure, backup and data recovery, network and security, and storage. Customer/partner manages annual maintenance.	Customers are in control of deployment and maintenance with their own dedicated IT infrastructure and staff. Customer/partner manages annual maintenance.
Implementation approach	SAP provides predefined best practice configuration with limited customization using the SAP Activate methodology.	SAP Activate is available, but not required. Best practices are available for selected countries.	The implementation approach is based on the specific requirements regarding business process and customization.	The implementation approach is based on the specific requirements regarding business process and customization.

(continued)

Table 13-1. (*continued*)

	SAP S/4HANA Cloud	SAP S/4HANA Cloud Single-Tenant	SAP S/4HANA Private Cloud Hosted	SAP S/4HANA On-Premise
Speed of implementation	Relatively fast to implement as it leverages a ready-made platform that has already been provisioned, implemented, and tested by SAP.	Slower than multitenant but faster than on-premise. The solution leverages SAP Model Company and SAP provides services for infrastructure, environment provisioning, and upgrades.	The customer can directly start the On-Premise Edition implementation on the hosted model without any up-front cost or commitment for storage or network infrastructure. Subscription costs are to be paid to the hosting vendor.	Takes time, resources, and infrastructure to set up a new environment. Additional hardware and software purchases might be needed.
Custom code and enhancements	In-app extensibility with limited ABAP or side-by-side extensibility; SAP Cloud Platform as an extension platform for the customization.	All custom coding is possible in SAP Cloud Platform except for SAP source code modifications.	Traditional ABAP extensibility limited up to core functionality modifications.	Traditional ABAP extensibility limited up to core functionality modifications.

System upgrade	Automatic quarterly innovation upgrades.	Twice-annual innovation upgrade cycle; subject to customer discretion.	The customer is responsible for the system upgrade and any necessary system changes, with hosted vendor support.	The customer has full control over planned downtime and changes within the system. SAP does not provide upgrades.
Innovation cycle and version	Innovation and feature upgrades are done quarterly.	One major upgrade per year aligned with SAP S/4HANA code-line, which is required to be accepted, and one feature pack upgrade per year.	One major upgrade per year aligned with SAP S/4HANA code-line, which is optional. The customer is responsible for the system upgrade and any necessary system changes, with hosted vendor support.	One major upgrade per year aligned with SAP S/4HANA code-line, which is optional. The customer is responsible for the system upgrade and any necessary system changes.

(continued)

Table 13-1. (*continued*)

	SAP S/4HANA Cloud	SAP S/4HANA Cloud Single-Tenant	SAP S/4HANA Private Cloud Hosted	SAP S/4HANA On-Premise
Deployment options	Phased deployments are required due to the sequential configuration by region/country.	Phased and simultaneous approaches supported.	Phased as well as synchronous approaches supported.	Phased and synchronous approaches supported.
TCO (Total Cost of Ownership)	Lowest	Lower	Moderate	Highest

Additional References

- https://blogs.sap.com/2018/07/28/the-5-golden-
  rules-for-implementing-sap-s4hana-cloud-single-
  tenant-edition/

- https://blogs.sap.com/2017/12/28/sap-s4-hana-
  central-finance-a-complete-understanding-about-
  central-finance/

Index

E

V, W, X, Y, Z

Printed in the United States
By Bookmasters